To:

_____

From:

_____

May my prayer be set before you like incense;
may the lifting up of my hands be like
the evening sacrifice.

Psalm *141:2*

In This Quiet Place
Copyright 1999 by ZondervanPublishingHouse
ISBN 0-310-97900-5

Requests for information should be addressed to :

🔖 ZondervanPublishingHouse
Mail Drop B20
Grand Rapids, Michigan 49530
http://www.zondervan.com

Senior Editor: Gwen Ellis
Project Editor: Traci Mullins
Designer: John Lucas

Printed in China

00 01/HK/3

In This Quiet Place

*Discovering the Pleasure
of Prayer*

In This Quiet Place

The
Gift
of
Prayer

Wealth and riches are in his house,
and his righteousness endures forever.

Psalm *112:3*

I have found that prayer is the most wonderful gift in
God's great bag of blessings. It is the great adventure
of the Christian faith. No matter who we are or what
our life circumstances may be, prayer can become for
us a thrilling, daily adventure. So many of us are need-
lessly living at a level far beneath that which God
wants for us. He has a storehouse full of rich provi-
sions, just waiting to be distributed to all those who
will simply ask Him to open His hand. So often it is
true that we have not because we ask not.

David Jeremiah

I will give you the treasures of darkness,
riches stored in secret places,
so that you may know that I am the LORD,
the God of Israel, who summons you by name.

Isaiah *45:3*

Prayer is a most precious thing, for it is the channel by which priceless blessings come to believers and the window through which their needs are supplied by a gracious God. Prayer is the vessel that trades with heaven and comes home from the celestial country laden with treasure of far greater worth than ever Spanish galleon brought from the land of gold.

Charles Spurgeon

I pray also that the eyes of your heart may be enlightened in order that you may know the hope to which he has called you, the riches of his glorious inheritance in the saints, and his incomparably great power for us who believe. That power is like the working of his mighty strength, which he exerted in Christ when he raised him from the dead and seated him at his right hand in the heavenly realms, far above all rule and authority, power and dominion, and every title that can be given, not only in the present age but also in the one to come. And God placed all things under his feet and appointed him to be head over everything for the church, which is his body, the fullness of him who fills everything in every way.

Ephesians 1:18–23

The Great Adventure

Two things are said to be certain —death and taxes. Let me add a third — problems. But unlike the first two, you can do something about the latter. You can pray. In his love, God has provided prayer as a means to forge fellowship with himself and provide access to his wisdom for our problems. God is in the problem-solving business, and when you present your dilemmas to him, he will answer. His reply may not be what you thought or wanted, and it may not fit neatly into your schedule. Nonetheless, God has entered into a covenant relationship with you whereby he assumes the awesome responsibility to help you, lead you, correct you, and make his will known to you. Prayer is the frontier of discover.

Charles F. Stanley

Oh, the depth of the riches of the wisdom and knowledge of God!
How unsearchable his judgments,
and his paths beyond tracing out!
"Who has known the mind of the Lord?
Or who has been his counselor?"
"Who has ever given to God,
that God should repay him?"
For from him and through him and to him are all things.
To him be the glory forever! Amen.

Romans *11:33–36*

We're Made for God

We pray because it is our most human response. We're made by and for the voice of God—listening to and answering that voice is our most characteristic act. We are most ourselves when we pray.

Eugene H. Peterson

In every circumstance of life, prayer is the most natural outpouring of the soul, the unhindered turning to God for communion and direction. Whether in sorrow or in joy, in defeat or in victory, in weakness or in health, in calamity or in success, the heart leaps to meet with God, just as a child runs to his mother's arms, ever sure that her sympathy will meet every need.

E. M. Bounds

You are great, Lord, and greatly to be praised. Great is your power, and of your wisdom there is no end. And man, who is part of what you have created, desires to praise you. For you have stirred up his heart so that he takes pleasure in praising you. You have created us for yourself, and our hearts are restless until they rest in you.

St. Augustine

What a Friend!

Christians know that for them prayer is as essential as
breathing, and once they have tasted the sweetness of
intimate conversation with God, they do not hesitate to
immerse themselves in it with trusting abandonment.

Pope John Paul II

What a Friend we have in Jesus, all our sins and griefs to bear!
What a privilege to carry everything to God in prayer!
O what peace we often forfeit, O what needless pain we bear,
All because we do not carry everything to God in prayer!

Have we trials and temptations? Is there trouble anywhere?
We should never be discouraged, take it to the Lord in prayer.
Can we find a friend so faithful who will all our sorrows share?
Jesus knows our every weakness, take it to the Lord in prayer.

Are we weak and heavy-laden, cumbered with a load of care?
Precious Saviour, still our refuge —take it to the Lord in prayer.
Do thy friends despise, forsake thee? Take it to the Lord in prayer.
In His arms He'll take and shield thee, thou wilt find a solace there.

Joseph Scriven

*Loving Father, faithful and full of power, I'm so grateful
I can come to You with confidence, for You keep
Your promises and answer prayer. Not one single
word of Your good promises has ever failed.
Lord, I submit myself to You, presenting my life and my
desires as a living sacrifice. I acknowledge You as Lord of
my desires, my plans, my successes and failures, my place
in the world, my friendships, my popularity. You are Lord
of my present and future relationships, health, money, pos-
sessions, and human approval. How good it is to yield to
You, knowing that You withhold no good thing from Your
obedient children who trust You and call on You.*

Warren and Ruth Myers

The Divine Welcome

Prayer is not a reward we deserve but a *privilege* given by God. It is His gift to us, not our gift to Him. There is no doubt about God's unwavering love for His children. He wants to hear from us not because we are deserving, but because it simply pleases Him to do so.

William Carr Peel

Prayer has mostly to do with God. His grace. His willingness. His invitation. What we say in our devotional times is our response to God's invitation. Prayer is not some bright idea *we've* thought of. In Jesus Christ, God opened the door. In prayer we walk through.

Timothy Jones

God is greater than your problem and is eminently able to resolve it. The power of prayer can never be overestimated because of the omnipotent God who hears and answers. Be willing to work out your difficulty his way, follow his instructions, and assume the risk that he may or may not remove the problem. In any case, your petitions will set the stage for the best possible solution, for you have put your trust in the God who cares.

Charles F. Stanley

They feast on the abundance of your house;
you give them drink from your river of delights.

Psalm *36:8*

Dear Lord, it seems that you are so madly in love with
your creatures that you could not live without us. So
you created us; and then, when we turned away from
you, you redeemed us. Yet you are God, and so have no
need of us. Your greatness is made no greater by our creation; your power is made no stronger by our redemption. You have no duty to care for us, no debt to re-pay
us. It is love, and love alone, which moves you.

Catherine of Siena

The LORD delights in those who fear him,
who put their hope in his unfailing love.

Psalm *147:11*

Instant Access

The greatest privilege God gives to you is the freedom
to approach Him at any time. You are not only authorized to speak to Him; you are invited. You are not
only permitted; you are expected. God waits for you to
communicate with Him. You have instant, direct
access to God. God loves mankind so much, and in a
very special sense His children, that He has made
Himself available to you at all times.

As a child of God you have full authority to contact
God, the Sovereign of the universe, whenever you
desire. He is always enthroned in heaven; yet, through
prayer, you have as much access to His presence as any
angel or archangel. You need not wait for an invitation; the invitation is already yours. You need not
make a prior appointment; you are already authorized
to approach God instantly. God is never too busy to
listen to you; He is never too involved to answer you.

Wesley L. Duewel

Let us then approach the throne of grace with confidence, so that we may receive mercy and find grace to
help us in our time of need.

Hebrews 4:16

O LORD, our LORD,
how majestic is your name in all the earth!

You have set your glory
above the heavens.
From the lips of children and infants
you have ordained praise
because of your enemies,
to silence the foe and the avenger.

When I consider your heavens,
the work of your fingers,
the moon and the stars,
which you have set in place,
what is man that you are mindful of him,
the son of man that you care for him?
You made him a little lower than the heavenly beings
and crowned him with glory and honor.

You made him ruler over the works of your hands;
you put everything under his feet:
all flocks and herds,
and the beasts of the field,
the birds of the air,
and the fish of the sea,
all that swim the paths of the seas.

O LORD, our LORD,
how majestic is your name in all the earth!

Psalm 8

We Are God's Delight

Contrary to what most of us imagine, prayer did not originate with us, but it began with God Himself. His unique self-disclosure, given to us so freely in His Word, reveals that His very being is one of utter love. Out of this supernatural self-giving and self-sharing, there flows His divine desire to have children with whom He can share His very life. He dotes over us with unfailing compassion and infinite mercy, drawing us to Himself with loving care. He delights to draw near to us so that we, in response to His presence, can commune with Him, enjoy Him, trust Him. This is prayer!

W. Phillip Keller

The LORD your God is with you,
he is mighty to save.
He will take great delight in you,
he will quiet you with his love,
he will rejoice over you with singing.

Zephaniah 3:17

Any true life of the spirit must be narrated as a story of God's search for humankind, not humankind's search for God. God makes the first move; he understands our being and is conversant with our most personal inner life. His seeking removes all the panic from faith and all the anxiety from hope.

Eugene H. Peterson

The Bible reveals a God Who, long before it even occurs to man to turn to Him, while man is still lost in darkness and sunk in sin, takes the initiative, rises from His throne, lays aside His glory, and stoops to seek until He finds him.

John R. W. Stott

Jesus, being in very nature God,
did not consider equality with God something to be grasped,
but made himself nothing,
taking the very nature of a servant,
being made in human likeness.
And being found in appearance as a man,
he humbled himself
and became obedient to death —
even death on a cross!
Therefore God exalted him to the highest place
and gave him the name that is above every name,
that at the name of Jesus every knee should bow,
in heaven and on earth and under the earth,
and every tongue confess that Jesus Christ is Lord,
to the glory of God the Father.

Philippians *2:6-11*

The Soul's Longing

Prayer is the conversation we have with God. As in any conversation, sometimes we communicate what's in our heart with great articulation, even eloquence. Other times we find only a toy box of childish expressions. Still other times we grope for words the way a newborn gropes for its mother's breast.

But the expression of our longing is not as important as the longing itself. For prayer is nothing more than the soul's longing for God —and the words nothing more than a child's attempt to describe them.

Ken Gire

O God, you are my God,
earnestly I seek you;
my soul thirsts for you,
my body longs for you,
in a dry and weary land
where there is no water.

I have seen you in the sanctuary
and beheld your power and your glory.
Because your love is better than life,
my lips will glorify you.
I will praise you as long as I live,
and in your name I will lift up my hands.
My soul will be satisfied as with the richest of foods;
with singing lips my mouth will praise you.

Psalm 63:1-5

A Holy Privilege

Jesus said, "I no longer call you servants, because a servant does not know his master's business. Instead, I have called you friends, for everything that I learned from my Father I have made known to you."

John 15:15

At the moment Jesus Christ died, untouched by a human hand, the curtain of the temple that separated man from the presence of God was torn from top to bottom. For the first time a priest performing rituals before that thick temple curtain could see right into the holiest place of all. It was like looking into the face of God. That torn curtain was the symbol of ability to access the throne of God. It gave the children of God the holy privilege of walking straight into his presence. That privilege remains today and is available to anyone who through prayer approaches the throne of grace.

M.G. Ellis

If we will, we can turn any radio or T.V. newscast or newspaper article into a call to prayer. We can be alert to share God's heartbeat for a broken world. Prayer is the supreme way to be workers together with God.

Wesley L. Duewel

God has willingly chosen to act through us and through our asking. God wants to enlist us in his plans, inviting us to participate through prayer. Of course he is powerful enough not to have to call on our puny muscle and stuttering prayers, and he already knows what we tell him. But for our sakes and for the sake of others he becomes the Great Delegator. He allows us to participate with him in what is and what is to come.

In so many ways God seems to prefer to work through the slow, the steady, the *human*, rather than through fiat and thunderclap. In prayer we take hold of his willingness to listen and move; we exercise our right as children to influence a loving parent. When I stop to consider the opportunity he gives us, it marshals forth a palpable thirst to ask. Think of it! *We can make a difference.*

The world does not face an impersonal fate; God is on the move, and he's enlisting us in his kingdom's advance.

Timothy Jones

God Is Near

Wherever you work, you can pray. Wherever you lie, you can pray. There is no place to which you can be banished where God is not near, and there is no time of day or night when His throne is inaccessible.

Charles Spurgeon

Anything that is of concern to you is fair grounds for prayer. The power and beauty of prayer will come shining through in the specificity of your praying. God will cease to be "out there" or "up there" and will come to reside in your everyday life. God will not be Creator only but will become Companion.

Steve Harper

The best reason to pray is that God is really there. In praying, our unbelief gradually starts to melt. God moves smack into the middle of even an ordinary day. He is no longer someone we theorize about. He is someone we want to be near.

Emilie Griffin

The LORD is gracious and compassionate,
slow to anger and rich in love.
The LORD is good to all;
he has compassion on all he has made. . .

The LORD is faithful to all his promises
and loving toward all he has made.
The LORD upholds all those who fall
and lifts up all who are bowed down.
The eyes of all look to you,
and you give them their food at the proper time.
You open your hand
and satisfy the desires of every living thing.

The LORD is righteous in all his ways
and loving toward all he has made.
The LORD is near to all who call on him,
to all who call on him in truth.
He fulfills the desires of those who fear him;
he hears their cry and saves them.
The LORD watches over all who love him,
but all the wicked he will destroy.

Psalm *145:8-9, 13-20*

Dare to Believe

It is beyond the capacity of the human mind to understand how big, how vast, how glorious, how grand, and how beautiful God is. And yet from His grandeur, magnificence, and size, God comes to touch the heart of any person who turns to Him in faith.

And with all of His splendor and grandeur, God is also a God of details. Scripture tells us He knows the number of hairs on our heads. He cares for the lilies of the field and for every sparrow, yet He cares for us much more than that. God is interested in the details of your life. He knows exactly where you are at this moment and He knows every problem you face. He knows your frustrations. He knows when you are hoping against hope.

Dare to believe that God does love you. Believe it against all odds. Dream against all dreams that God does care about you and has a plan for your life and wants you to succeed. Look to God when the reports are bad, when there appears to be no hope. And as you hope against hope, God will hear your prayers.

Robert A. Schuller

Mustard–Seed Faith

Early in the morning, as he [Jesus] was on his way back to the city, he was hungry. Seeing a fig tree by the road, he went up to it but found nothing on it except leaves. Then he said to it, "May you never bear fruit again!" Immediately the tree withered. When the disciples saw this, they were amazed. "How did the fig tree wither so quickly?" they asked. Jesus replied, "I tell you the truth, if you have faith and do not doubt, not only can you do what was done to the fig tree, but also you can say to this mountain, 'Go, throw yourself into the sea,' and it will be done. If you believe, you will receive whatever you ask for in prayer."

Matthew *21:18–22*

The apostles said to the Lord, "Increase our faith!" He replied, "If you have faith as small as a mustard seed, you can say to this mulberry tree, 'Be uprooted and planted in the sea,' and it will obey you."

Luke *17:5–6*

God does not require you to have great faith. You simply are to have faith in a great God.

Bill Bright

Our Ever-Present God

O LORD, you have searched me
and you know me.
You know when I sit and when I rise;
you perceive my thoughts from afar.
You discern my going out and my lying down;
you are familiar with all my ways.
Before a word is on my tongue
you know it completely, O LORD.

You hem me in —behind and before;
you have laid your hand upon me.
Such knowledge is too wonderful for me,
too lofty for me to attain.

Where can I go from your Spirit?
Where can I flee from your presence?
If I go up to the heavens, you are there;
if I make my bed in the depths, you are there.
If I rise on the wings of the dawn,
if I settle on the far side of the sea,
even there your hand will guide me,
your right hand will hold me fast.

If I say, "Surely the darkness will hide me
and the light become night around me,"
even the darkness will not be dark to you;
the night will shine like the day,
for darkness is as light to you.

For you created my inmost being;
you knit me together in my mother's womb.
I praise you because I am fearfully and wonderfully
made;
your works are wonderful,
I know that full well.
My frame was not hidden from you
when I was made in the secret place.
When I was woven together in the depths of the earth,
your eyes saw my unformed body.
All the days ordained for me
were written in your book
before one of them came to be.

How precious to me are your thoughts, O God!
How vast is the sum of them!
Were I to count them,
they would outnumber the grains of sand.
When I awake,
I am still with you.

Psalm *139:1-18*

"Lord,
Teach
Us to
Pray"

Praying Like Jesus

Jesus [prayed] in private and in public. He prayed in the Temple and in the synagogues. He prayed in homes and on the open road. He prayed at funerals and at parties. He prayed in the Garden of Gethsemane, and he prayed from the cross. He prayed in nearly all the possible locations of his time. Jesus [prayed] early in the morning and late at night. Sometimes he would pray briefly; at other times he spent hours in prayer. When [he] gave the Lord's Prayer, he had just finished a time of his own private praying. For Jesus, the time might be short or long, but anytime was prayer time.

Steve Harper

Jesus said, "And when you pray, do not be like the hypocrites, for they love to pray standing in the synagogues and on the street corners to be seen by men. I tell you the truth, they have received their reward in full. But when you pray, go into your room, close the door and pray to your Father, who is unseen. Then your Father, who sees what is done in secret, will reward you."

Matthew 6:5–6

Prayer is the soul's sincere desire,
Uttered or unexpressed,
The motion of a hidden fire
That trembles in the breast.

Prayer is the simplest form of speech
That infant lips can try;
Prayer the sublimest strains that reach
The majesty on high.

Prayer is the contrite sinner's voice
Returning from his ways,
While angels in their songs rejoice,
And cry: "Behold, he prays!"

Prayer is the Christian's vital breath,
The Christian's native air,
Our watchword at the gate of death;
We enter heaven with prayer.

O thou by whom we come to God,
The Life, the Truth, the Way!
The path of prayer thyself hast trod:
Lord, teach us how to pray!

James Montgomery

Come Away with Me

Very early in the morning, while it was still dark, Jesus got up, left the house and went off to a solitary place, where he prayed. Simon and his companions went to look for him, and when they found him, they exclaimed: "Everyone is looking for you!"

Mark 1:35-37

At daybreak Jesus went out to a solitary place.

Luke 4:42

Immediately Jesus made the disciples get into the boat and go on ahead of him to the other side, while he dismissed the crowd. After he had dismissed them, he went up on a mountainside by himself to pray. When evening came, he was there alone.

Matthew 14:22-23

One of those days Jesus went out to a mountainside to pray, and spent the night praying to God.

Luke 6:12

My Child,

When the world and its chaos closes in on you, do as Jesus did: Run to me in prayer. For only in the solitary world of prayer can you be equipped to live in the crowded world of others. In the solitude I will siphon off the poisons of resentment and jealousy, covetousness and fear. In the solitude I will fuel you with my mercy and gentleness, my patience and grace. And as you return day after day to the peace and solitude of prayer, you will begin to find yourself more and more able to carry that peace and solitude away with you, back into the noisy, crowded world, like a turtle carries its home upon its back.

Come away with me,

Abba

Claire Cloninger

Jesus said, "Come to me, all you who are weary and burdened, and I will give you rest. Take my yoke upon you and learn from me, for I am gentle and humble in heart, and you will find rest for your souls. For my yoke is easy and my burden is light."

Matthew *11:28–30*

Ask...

[Jesus] said to [his disciples], "Suppose one of you has a friend, and he goes to him at midnight and says, 'Friend, lend me three loaves of bread, because a friend of mine on a journey has come to me, and I have nothing to set before him.' Then the one inside answers, 'Don't bother me. The door is already locked, and my children are with me in bed. I can't get up and give you anything.' I tell you, though he will not get up and give him the bread because he is his friend, yet because of the man's boldness he will get up and give him as much as he needs. So I say to you: Ask and it will be given to you; seek and you will find; knock and the door will be opened to you. For everyone who asks receives; he who seeks finds; and to him who knocks, the door will be opened."

Luke *11:5-10*

Some people think God does not like to be troubled with our constant asking. The way to trouble God is not to come at all.

Dwight L. Moody

Asking is a way of life with an open hand. To ask is to depend on someone other than yourself. It is very humbling. Asking indicates: I don't know. I failed. I ran out. I can't find it. I'm not sure. I don't understand. I forgot. I didn't listen. I didn't care. I was wrong. I'm not prepared. I need more information. I came up short.

That's why Jesus says we should ask. Asking puts us back on track with God. It assumes we need a relationship with Him —a hand-to-mouth spiritual existence. A vulnerable daily dependence. In a society that rushes to fill every felt need, that steals away the soul of a person and offers to sell it back at a price, we need to rekindle what it means to ask God.

Ask, Jesus says. Ask. It's so simple —like a child. Ask. And when you receive, keep on asking. Don't accept a fake fill. Live in your thirst and you will live in Him. Open your hand. Ask.

John Fisher

Jesus said, "Until now you have not asked for anything in my name. Ask and you will receive, and your joy will be complete."

John *16:24*

Seek...

There are no cat-and-mouse games to be played in prayer. If we seek Him, He promises our efforts won't be in vain.

Joni Eareckson Tada

But if you seek the LORD your God, you will find him if you look for him with all your heart and with all your soul.

Deuteronomy 4:29

Those who know your name will trust in you,
for you, LORD, have never forsaken those who seek you.

Psalm 9:10

The lions may grow weak and hungry,
but those who seek the LORD lack no good thing.

Psalm 34:10

Glory in his holy name;
let the hearts of those who seek the LORD rejoice.
Look to the LORD and his strength;
seek his face always.

1 Chronicles *16:10-11*

One thing I ask of the LORD,
this is what I seek:
that I may dwell in the house of the LORD
all the days of my life,
to gaze upon the beauty of the LORD
and to seek him in his temple. . .
My heart says of you, "Seek his face!"
Your face, LORD, I will seek.

Psalm *27:4, 8*

Knock...

Then Jesus told his disciples a parable to show them that they should always pray and not give up. He said: "In a certain town there was a judge who neither feared God nor cared about men. And there was a widow in that town who kept coming to him with the plea, 'Grant me justice against my adversary.' For some time he refused. But finally he said to himself, 'Even though I don't fear God or care about men, yet because this widow keeps bothering me, I will see that she gets justice, so that she won't eventually wear me out with her coming!'" And the Lord said, "Listen to what the unjust judge says. And will not God bring about justice for his chosen ones, who cry out to him day and night? Will he keep putting them off? I tell you, he will see that they get justice, and quickly."

Luke 18:1-8

The strongest one in Christ's kingdom is he who can knock the best.

E. M. Bounds

When our son was growing up, he asked again and again for a motorbike. He plastered a picture of one on our refrigerator, just in case we forgot what he wanted. He was insistent around the clock. Like a perpetual motion machine, he asked and asked. No one had to teach John to persevere.

Christians need that kind of persistence in prayer — the ability to keep on keeping on in spite of discouragement or doubt. Effective prayer is seldom a sprint; it's a marathon.

James & Martha Reapsome

According to Jesus, by far the most important thing about praying is to keep at it. Be importunate, Jesus says —not, one assumes, because you have to beat a path to God's door before he'll open it, but because until you beat the path maybe there's no way of getting to *your* door.

Frederick Buechner

The Lord is glad to open the gate to every knocking soul. It opens very freely; its hinges are not rusted, no bolts secure it. Have faith and enter at this moment through holy courage. If you knock with a heavy heart, you shall yet sing with joy of spirit. Never be discouraged!

Charles Spurgeon

Come and listen, all you who fear God;
    let me tell you what he has done for me.
I cried out to him with my mouth;
    his praise was on my tongue.
If I had cherished sin in my heart,
    The Lord would not have listened;
but God has surely listened
    and heard my voice in prayer.
Praise be to God,
    who has not rejected my prayer
or withheld his love from me!

Psalm 66: 16–20

The Lord's Prayer

And it came to pass, that as he was praying in a certain place, when he ceased, one of his disciples said unto him, "Lord, teach us to pray, as John alslo taught his disciples." And he said unto them, "When ye pray, say:

Our Father which art in heaven, Hallowed be thy name.

Thy kingdom come. Thy will be done in earth, as it is in heaven.

Give us this day our daily bread.

And forgive us our debts, as we forgive our debtors.

And lead us not into temptation, but deliver us from evil: For thine is the kingdom,

and the power, and the glory, for ever. Amen.

Luke *11:1-2*, KJV; Matthew *6:9-13*, KJV

"Lord, teach us to pray." When, on the slopes of the Mount of Olives, the apostles addressed Jesus with these words they were not asking an ordinary question, but with spontaneous trust, they were expressing one of the deepest needs of the human heart.

Pope John Paul II

Sometimes life looks like the backside of a loom. A day's circumstances seem as disconnected as the threads on the underside of an Oriental rug. We are hard pressed to see any pattern or purpose to it all. Prayer is the Divine Weaver's invitation to step around to what is really the front side of the loom, to the eternal side of life. And the movement is transformational, often breathtaking. The upward look of prayer reveals the real meaning of life.

In giving us the Lord's Prayer, Jesus was inviting us to step around the loom and see life from the perspective of heaven. True prayer is God's invitation to see life through God's eyes and to set the circumstances of life in their larger context. We need this perspective if we are to see our lives as more than a disconnected sequence of events.

Jesus was able to put it all into perspective. And as he looked at the cross itself, he was able to say, "It was for this that I came into the world."

Steve Harper

Our Father in Heaven...

Jesus declared that instead of praying only at set times in the synagogue, instead of using the words of their ancestors and prophets, people could now talk directly with Yahweh, the Lord of All, the Feared One. They could call Him *Daddy*.

Dudley Delffs

Jesus spent his whole ministry trying to get his followers to know the God he called "Abba." His little roadside "theology courses" painted God not as some far-off, inaccessible deity, but as a Shepherd who searched tirelessly for a lost sheep, as a loving Dad who waited with forgiveness on his lips to welcome home a wayward child. These stories are simple but powerful lessons that call us into the waiting arms of a great mercy.

In fact, the whole redemptive mission of Jesus might be viewed as making a way for us to come into his Abba's presence with childlike confidence. He was, in a sense, placing the small hand of humanity in the great, kind hand of its Creator and saying, "Child, come, and know your Father."

Claire Cloninger

To say that God is in heaven does not imply absence from earth. Rather, it says, "God is in the right place, doing the right things." God is not capricious or inconsistent, nor is God one who may or may not be there when we pray. God *is* in heaven, *is* in charge. No matter when we pray, we can count on that.

Steve Harper

I lift up my eyes to the hills —
where does my help come from?
My help comes from the LORD,
the Maker of heaven and earth.

He will not let your foot slip —
he who watches over you will not slumber;
indeed, he who watches over Israel
will neither slumber nor sleep.

The LORD watches over you —
the LORD is your shade at your right hand;
the sun will not harm you by day,
nor the moon by night.

The LORD will keep you from all harm —
he will watch over your life;
the LORD will watch over your coming and going
both now and forevermore.

Psalm *121*

Hallowed Be Your Name...

Our Father in heaven, may your name be honoured. That is, may you be worshipped by your whole creation; may the whole cosmos resound with your praise; may the whole world be freed from injustice, disfigurement, sin, and death. And as we stand in the presence of the living God, with the darkness and pain of the world on our hearts, praying that he will fulfill his ancient promises, and implement the victory of Calvary and Easter for the whole Cosmos —then we may discover that our own pain, our own darkness, is somehow being dealt with as well.

N. T. Wright

I will exalt you, my God the King;
I will praise your name for ever and ever.
Every day I will praise you
and extol your name for ever and ever.

Great is the LORD and most worthy of praise;
his greatness no one can fathom.

Psalm *145:1-3*

Your Kingdom Come...

When you pray "Thy kingdom come," you are saying, "God, You are the King. You live in my heart. And I want Your kingdom principles and purposes to be lived out within me, as You reign within me. I know the manifest, visible kingdom isn't here on this earth yet, but there can be a little touch of the kingdom within me as I walk with You and talk with You and live for You each day." God has called us to live as if the King were already in residence on this earth, because He does reside in our hearts.

David Jeremiah

Christ envisaged His own future kingdom on earth and also the very Spirit of the living God coming into the human heart to make it His holy habitation. He saw a human being as a temple, an abode, a residence of the Most High.

The peace which we enjoy in God's Kingdom surpasses any sort of mere outward tranquility. It is that deep, delightful serenity of soul characteristic of God's presence. It is based upon being at peace with God, at peace with others, and at peace with ourselves.

W. Phillip Keller

Your Will Be Done on Earth as It Is in Heaven...

We are praying, as Jesus was praying and acting, for the redemption of the world; for the radical defeat and uprooting of evil; and for heaven and earth to be married at last, for God to be all in all.

N. T. Wright

The sooner a child of God discovers the great delight of moving in harmony with the will of God, the sooner he has set his feet on the threshold of heaven. For it is in doing the will of God and responding to it positively that heaven actually does descend to this fragment of earth and becomes a reality within.

God's will carries within it all that has been set in motion for our welfare and benefit. He has our best interests at heart. So to do His will is really to do ourselves as well as Him a great favor. The final result is to find ourselves in complete accord and harmony with the will of our Father in heaven. And to experience joy, serenity, usefulness, worth, and enormous adventure in our walk with God as we move in accord with His plans and purposes on this planet.

W. Phillip Keller

Then Jesus went with his disciples to a place called
Gethsemane, and he said to them, "Sit here while I go
over there and pray." He took Peter and the two sons
of Zebedee along with him, and he began to be sor-
rowful and troubled. Then he said to them, "My soul
is overwhelmed with sorrow to the point of death.
Stay here and keep watch with me."

Going a little farther, he fell with his face to the
ground and prayed, "My Father, if it is possible, may
this cup be taken from me. Yet not as I will, but as
you will.". . .

He went away a second time and prayed, "My
Father, if it is not possible for this cup to be taken
away unless I drink it, may your will be done."

Matthew *26:36–39, 42*

Meanwhile his disciples urged him, "Rabbi, eat something." But he said to them, "I have food to eat that
you know nothing about." Then his disciples said to
each other, "Could someone have brought him food?"
"My food," said Jesus, "is to do the will of him who
sent me and to finish his work.

John *4:31–34*

Give Us Today Our Daily Bread...

If we were not so familiar with the Lord's Prayer, we would be astonished at the petition for daily bread. If it had come from the lips of any other than Jesus himself, we would consider it an intrusion of materialism upon the refined realm of prayer. But here it is smack in the middle of the greatest of prayers.

When we think about it, though, we realize that this prayer is completely consistent with Jesus' pattern of living, for he occupied himself with the trivialities of humankind. He provided wine for those who were celebrating, food for those who were hungry, rest for those who were weary. He went out of his way to find the "little people": the poor, the sick, the powerless.

Richard J. Foster

Prayer wears denim work clothes. It is about day-to-day living. Prayer is about everyday things, about bread and about money. Prayer is about real-world concerns, spoken in real-world language. God does not want us to shift into a stained-glass prayer voice to address Him. Prayer comes out of this world, the workaday world of houses and cars and sewer lines and schools and janitors and the IRS.

David Jeremiah

Forgive Us Our Debts, as We Also Have Forgiven Our Debtors...

To pray this prayer is to pray for the world: lift up your eyes for a moment, away from your own sins and those of your immediate neighbour, and see the world as a whole, groaning in travail, longing for peace and justice; see the endless tangles in which politicians and power-brokers get themselves, and the endless human misery which results; of the men of violence who have forgotten that there was a different way to live. Collect all these images and roll them into one, that of a young Jewish boy off in the far country feeding the pigs; and then, with your courage in both hands, say, "Forgive us our trespasses": "I will arise and go to my father, and will say to him, Father, I have sinned...." But, as you say it, with the whole world of pain in view, allow your praying heart to see the next scene, with the Father doing the unthinkable, the disgraceful thing, and running down the road to meet his muddled and muddy son.

N. T. Wright

And when you stand praying, if you hold anything against anyone, forgive him, so that your Father in heaven may forgive you your sins.

Mark 11:25

[Jesus] teaches us this way because he knows how very much God loves to forgive. It is the one thing he yearns to do, aches to do, rushes to do. At the very heart of the universe is God's desire to give and to forgive.

Richard J. Foster

Joseph's brothers said, "What if Joseph holds a grudge against us and pays us back for all the wrongs we did to him?". . . His brothers then came and threw themselves down before him. "We are your slaves," they said. But Joseph said to them, "Don't be afraid. Am I in the place of God? You intended to harm me, but God intended it for good to accomplish what is now being done, the saving of many lives. So then, don't be afraid. I will provide for you and your children." And he reassured them and spoke kindly to them.

Genesis *50:15, 18–21*

Lead Us Not into Temptation, but Deliver Us from the Evil One...

No temptation has seized you except what is common to man. And God is faithful; he will not let you be tempted beyond what you can bear. But when you are tempted, he will also provide a way out so that you can stand up under it.

1 Corinthians 10:13

In you, O LORD, I have taken refuge;
let me never be put to shame;
deliver me in your righteousness.
Turn your ear to me,
come quickly to my rescue;
be my rock of refuge,
a strong fortress to save me.
Since you are my rock and my fortress,
for the sake of your name lead and guide me.
Free me from the trap that is set for me,
for you are my refuge.

Psalm 31:1-4

Thanks be to God that, though you used to be slaves to sin, you wholeheartedly obeyed the form of teaching to which you were entrusted. You have been set free from sin and have become slaves to righteousness.

Romans 6:17-18

Our Master would not teach us to ask our heavenly Father for deliverance from evil if no deliverance was available. He would not instruct us to pray to be delivered from evil situations if our Father was unable to do so. But He *is*. And therein lies a great measure of the glory and joy of really knowing God as our Father. Let us never forget that our Father does not want to see us succumb to temptation. He does not want to see us fall. He does not want to see us down in despair, struggling with self, and stained by sin. He wants us, as His maturing children, to grow up in strength so we can walk serenely with Him in the beauty of a strong, unsullied, intimate companionship.

W. Phillip Keller

To him who is able to keep you from falling and to present you before his glorious presence without fault and with great joy —to the only God our Savior be glory, majesty, power and authority, through Jesus Christ our Lord, before all ages, now and forevermore! Amen.

Jude 24–25

Your Kingdom, Power, and Glory Forever!

Jesus said, "I have told you these things, so that in me you may have peace. In this world you will have trouble. But take heart! I have overcome the world."

John *16:33*

Jesus invites us to walk ahead into the darkness and discover that it, too, belongs to God. [And] when the darkness breaks it will be glory itself that wakes: wakes with the human cry of a small baby, blinking up at his mother in the sudden light, and seeing in her face, and reading in her heart, the hope and promise that God will triumph over fear, will deliver us from evil, and will bring in his kingdom at last.

N. T. Wright

David praised the Lord in the presence of the whole assembly, saying,. . .
"Yours, O Lord, is the greatness and the power
and the glory and the majesty and the splendor,
for everything in heaven and earth is yours.
Yours, O Lord, is the kingdom;
you are exalted as head over all. . . .
In your hands are strength and power
to exalt and give strength to all.
Now, our God, we give you thanks,
and praise your glorious name."

1 Chronicles *29:10-13*

All prayer concludes by placing everything in God's hands. Prayer may be filled with faith, uttered with boldness, offered in obedience and overflowing with praise and confidence. But after all is said, it's still up to Him. [Jesus] isn't saying, "Brace for a failure by casting yourself in a grand act of surrender." But He is teaching us this: "Your best finale is the declaration of His unchallengeable majesty. After you've worshiped and petitioned to the best of your Holy-Spirit-energized ability, rest it all with Him. The answers may not come in the size packages you suppose, or be delivered at the moment you have in mind. But trust Him. All power and glory are His. And in freely and praisefully speaking that, you open the door to His invitation that you share it with Him … in His way, at His time.

Jack Hayford

He who testifies to these things says, "Yes, I am coming soon."
Amen. Come, Lord Jesus.

Revelation *22:20*

To him who loves us and has freed us from our sins by his blood, and has made us to be a kingdom and priests to serve his God and Father —to him be glory and power for ever and ever! Amen.

Revelation *1:5-6*

Talking
to
Our
Father

"Abba, Father!"

But when the time had fully come, God sent his Son, born of a woman, born under law, to redeem those under law, that we might receive the full rights of sons. Because you are sons, God sent the Spirit of his Son into our hearts, the Spirit who calls out, *"Abba, Father."* So you are no longer a slave, but a son; and since you are a son, God has made you also an heir.

Galatians 4:4-7

Imagine your teenager walking up to you with this request, "O great and wise father, knower of all things, provider of my shelter and daily food, author of family order and peace, generous and benevolent ruler of the house, would you please lend me the car?" Not only would you think he was crazy, you would suspect he was up to something questionable.

When we speak to our heavenly Father in prayer, it should be as a child speaks to his earthly father. Prayer is simply *conversation between a child and his Father—verbal or non-verbal, formal or informal, public or private—concerning the topic of the child's choice.* Every newborn Christian can turn his thoughts toward Heaven to speak with his heavenly Father in prayer. It takes no special language, no specific formula, no certain place or posture. No topic is off limits. The child of God can pray *anywhere, any place, any time,* about *anything.*

William Carr Peel

Prayer is not acting a part of going through religious motions. Prayer is neither official nor formal nor ceremonial, but direct, hearty, intense. Prayer is the helpless and needy child crying to the compassion of the Father's heart and the bounty and power of the Father's hand. The answer is as sure to come as the Father's heart can be touched and the Father's hand be moved.

E. M. Bounds

Because the one to whom you pray is the King of kings and the Lord of lords, the Creator of heaven and earth, you come into His presence with reverence. But He is also your loving heavenly Father who cares for you and delights in having fellowship with you. Therefore, you can enter into His presence with a relaxed, joyful heart, knowing that God loves you more than anyone else has ever loved you or will ever love you.

Bill Bright

I have loved you with an everlasting love;
I have drawn you with loving-kindness.

Jeremiah 31:3

Baby Talk

I think this sweet word *Abba* was chosen to show us that we are to be very natural with God, not stilted and formal. We are to be very affectionate, to come close to Him and be bold to lie in His bosom, looking up into His face and speaking with holy boldness. "Abba" is not a word, somehow, but a babe's lisping. Oh, how near we are to God when we can use such speech! Be satisfied to offer to God broken language, words salted with your griefs, wetted with your tears. Go to Him with holy familiarity and be not afraid to cry in His presence, "Abba, Father."

Charles Spurgeon

People were also bringing babies to Jesus to have him touch them. When the disciples saw this, they rebuked them. But Jesus called the children to him and said, "Let the little children come to me, and do not hinder them, for the kingdom of God belongs to such as these. I tell you the truth, anyone who will not receive the kingdom of God like a little child will never enter it."

Luke *18:15–17*

God wants our hearts, and one of the essential ways we build our heart relationship with Him is through communication—deep, heart-level honest, engaging dialogues with Him. Prayer that comes from the hunger of our hearts ushers us into His presence like a child running to tell her father about her busy day. Our prayers become love letters home to our Abba Father. His response becomes a loving whisper in the world around us until that time when we can feel His breath in our ear and rest our head on His shoulder.

Dudley Delffs

My heart is not proud, O LORD,
my eyes are not haughty;
I do not concern myself with great matters
or things too wonderful for me.
But I have stilled and quieted my soul;
like a weaned child with its mother,
like a weaned child is my soul within me.

O Israel, put your hope in the LORD
both now and forevermore.

Psalm *131*

Come As You Are

God receives us just as we are and accepts our prayers just as they are. In the same way that a small child cannot draw a bad picture so a child of God cannot offer a bad prayer.

Richard J. Foster

Some of us are religiously jumpy and self-conscious because we know that God sees our every thought and is acquainted with all our ways. We need not be. God is the sum of all patience and the essence of kindly good will. We please Him most, not by frantically trying to make ourselves good, but by throwing ourselves into His arms with all our imperfections, and believing that He understands everything and loves us still.

A. W. Tozer

Come just as you are, opening your heart and telling Him how you feel and what you desire. You are God's child, and He is eager and willing to see you!

Wesley L. Duewel

Dear Child,

Prayer is a daily way of sharing your life with me. It's that simple. You don't have to be an expert on prayer to pray. I am not grading you like a teacher with a red pencil. I am not moved by intellectual words or poetic language. I just want to be with you. Release yourself from the need to achieve a great, impressive prayer life, and just give yourself permission to practice my presence. Be aware of how near I am to you. Talk to me as someone you trust. Take me into every situation. All that I ask for is your honesty. All that I long for is your company. Come to me. Bring your secret failures and your sad regrets. Bring your hopes and your happiness. Bring yourself to share with me. And you will find me waiting—a Father you can trust and a Friend you can depend on.

Ever your,
Abba

Claire Cloninger

Be Yourself

To some who were confident of their own righteousness and looked down on everybody else, Jesus told this parable: "Two men went up to the temple to pray, one a Pharisee and the other a tax collector. The Pharisee stood up and prayed about himself: 'God, I thank you that I am not like other men--robbers, evildoers, adulterers--or even like this tax collector. I fast twice a week and give a tenth of all I get.'

"But the tax collector stood at a distance. He would not even look up to heaven, but beat his breast and said, 'God, have mercy on me, a sinner.'

"I tell you that this man, rather than the other, went home justified before God. For everyone who exalts himself will be humbled, and he who humbles himself will be exalted."

Luke 18:9-14

The LORD is gracious and compassionate,
    slow to anger and rich in love.
The LORD is good to all;
    he has compassion on all he has made.
The LORD is righteous in all his ways
    and loving toward all he has made.
The LORD is near to all who call on him,
    to all who call on him in truth.

Psalm 145:8-9, 17-18

Tell Him Everything

Are you weary, are you heavy hearted?
Tell it to Jesus,
Tell it to Jesus;
Are you grieving over joys departed?
Tell it to Jesus alone.

Tell it to Jesus
Tell it to Jesus,
He is a friend that's well-known;
You've no other such a friend or brother,
Tell it to Jesus alone.

Jeremiah E. Rankin
1828 –1904—Baptist Hymnal

This is love: not that we loved God, but that he loved
us and sent his Son as an atoning sacrifice for our sins.

1 John *4:10*

The God of Little Things

Children do not find it difficult or complicated to talk to their parents, nor do they feel embarrassed to bring the simplest need to their attention. Neither should we hesitate to bring the simplest requests confidently to the Father.

Richard J. Foster

I have often felt that it takes more confidence in God to pray to Him about a little thing than about great things. We imagine that our great things are somehow worthy of God's attention, though in truth they are little enough to Him. And then we think that our little things must be so insignificant that it is an insult to bring them before Him.

We need to realize that what is very important to a child may be very small to his parent, and yet the parent measures the thing not from his own point of view but from the child's. God our Father is a good father who pities us as fathers pity their children. If you put your confidence in God, you will take your great things and little things to Him, knowing He will never belie your confidence.

Charles Spurgeon

Great is our Lord and mighty in power;
his understanding has no limit.
He heals the brokenhearted
and binds up their wounds.

Psalm *147:3, 5*

Imagine a little girl who comes crying to her mother
because her doll is broken. Her mother doesn't say,
"Come along, don't be silly; that doll isn't worth a
penny. What nonsense to cry about it." No, she
understands perfectly that the doll is the little one's
sweetheart, and she tries to comfort her and says, "Let
us look and see if we can mend the doll." Because she
loves, she sees the catastrophe through the eyes of the
child. God loves us more than an earthly father or
mother. And His love makes our problems great in His
eyes and small in our eyes.

Corrie ten Boom

As a father has compassion on his children,
so the LORD has compassion on those who fear him;
for he knows how we are formed,
he remembers that we are dust.

Psalm *103:13–14*

God Is Accessible

A special bond exists between [me and my children]. I'm their father! They can walk into my life any time they choose.

That's the way it is with our Father in heaven. You can go right into the presence of God Almighty and He will hear you. Incredible!

I have recently entered into a relationship with AT&T in my own fathering responsibilities. We gave our son a calling card and we got an 800 number. I said to Daniel a few days ago, "Son, I know there's a time difference between where we are and where you are, but I want you to know that, no matter what, any time you need to call us, *any time,* you can do it. I really mean that."

Now, if I am like that as an earthly father with limited resources, what do you think the Father in heaven is like? He owns the cattle on a thousand hills and you don't need a phone card or 800 number to reach Him. He's waiting for you to walk into His presence—ANY TIME. And He won't send you a bill.

David Jeremiah

The Antidote to Worry

The secret of Christian quietness is not indifference,
but the knowledge that God is my Father, He loves
me, I shall never think of anything He will forget, and
worry becomes an impossibility.

Oswald Chambers

Jesus said, "Do not worry about your life, what you
will eat or drink; or about your body, what you will
wear. Is not life more important than food, and the
body more important than clothes? Look at the birds
of the air; they do not sow or reap or store away in
barns, and yet your heavenly Father feeds them. Are
you not much more valuable than they? Who of you
by worrying can add a single hour to his life?"
"And why do you worry about clothes? See how the
lilies of the field grow. They do not labor or spin. Yet I
tell you that not even Solomon in all his splendor was
dressed like one of these. If that is how God clothes
the grass of the field, which is here today and tomorrow is thrown into the fire, will he not much more
clothe you, O you of little faith? So do not worry, saying, 'What shall we eat?' or 'What shall we drink?' or
'What shall we wear?' For the pagans run after all these
things, and your heavenly Father knows that you need
them. But seek first his kingdom and his righteousness, and all these things will be given to you as well."

Matthew *6:25-33*

"I Will Not Forget You"

Dear Child,

Open the eyes of your heart and see me as I am. I am the Father who longs to draw you near, to comfort you with tenderness when you are lonely or afraid, to shield you with care when you cry out to me, to shelter you and protect you as an eagle protects its young. Though this world is clouded with mixed messages and diluted commitments, my message is clear. My commitment is certain. I love you. You are mine. Though human love is not always consistent, my love is as sure as the sunrise. I am here for you and will be here. Though others may forget you, I never will. Your name has been carved into the palms of my open hands and your face is ever before me. You are my child.

I am your,
Abba

Claire Cloninger

For the LORD your God is a merciful God; he will not
abandon or destroy you or forget the covenant with
your forefathers, which he confirmed to them by oath.

Deuteronomy *4:31*

Shout for joy, O heavens;
rejoice, O earth;
burst into song, O mountains!
For the LORD comforts his people
and will have compassion on his afflicted ones. . . .

"Can a mother forget the baby at her breast
and have no compassion on the child she has borne?
Though she may forget,
I will not forget you!
See, I have engraved you on the palms of my hands;
your walls are ever before me."

Isaiah *49:13, 15–16*

But now, this is what the LORD says—
he who created you, O Jacob,
he who formed you, O Israel:
"Fear not, for I have redeemed you;
I have summoned you by name; you are mine."

Isaiah *43:1*

Boundless Mercy

Yet this I call to mind
and therefore I have hope:

Because of the LORD's great love
we are not consumed,
for his compassions never fail.
They are new every morning;
great is your faithfulness.

Lamentations *3:21–23*

Every morning mercies new
Fall as fresh as morning dew;
Every morning let us pay
Tribute with the early day:
For Thy mercies, Lord, are sure;
Thy compassion doth endure.

Greville Phillimore

Day by Day

Day by day, and with each passing moment,
Strength I find to meet my trials here;
Trusting in my Father's wise bestowment,
I've no cause for worry or for fear.
He whose heart is kind beyond all measure,
Gives unto each day what He deems best,
Lovingly it's part of pain and pleasure,
Mingling toil with peace and rest.

Ev'ry day the Lord Himself is near me,
With a special mercy for each hour;
All my cares He fain would bear and cheer me,
He whose name is Counsellor and Pow'r.
The protection of His child and treasure
Is a charge that on Himself He laid;
"As thy days, thy strength shall be in measure,"
This the pledge to me He made.

Help me then, in ev'ry tribulation,
So to trust Thy promises, O Lord.
That I lose not faith's sweet consolation,
Offered me within Thy holy word.
Help me, Lord, when toil and trouble meeting,
E'er to take, as from a father's hand,
One by one, the days, the moments fleeting,
Till I reach the promised land.

Lina Sandell

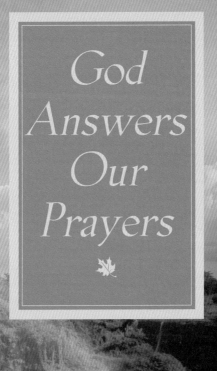

God
Answers
Our
Prayers

Gracious Inclinations

I love the LORD, for he heard my voice;
he heard my cry for mercy.
Because he turned his ear to me,
I will call on him as long as I live.

Psalm *116:1-2*

Every child of God may come before the King at all
times. The dead of night is not too late for God; the
breaking of the morning, when the first gray light is
seen, is not too early for the Most High; at midday He
is not too busy; and when the evening gathers He is not
too weary with His children's prayers. To pray continually is a most sweet and precious permit to the believer
to pour out his heart at all times before the Lord.

The doors of the temple of divine love shall not be
shut. Nothing can set a barrier between a praying soul
and its God. The road of angels and of prayers is ever
open. Let us but send out the dove of prayer and we
may be certain that she will return to us with an olive
branch of peace in her mouth. Evermore the Lord has
regard for the pleadings of His servants and waits to be
gracious to them.

Charles Spurgeon

The LORD longs to be gracious to you;
he rises to show you compassion.

Isaiah *30:18*

Evening, morning and noon
I cry out in distress,
and he hears my voice.
He ransoms me unharmed
from the battle waged against me,
even though many oppose me.

Psalm *55:17-18*

Find rest, O my soul, in God alone;
my hope comes from him.
He alone is my rock and my salvation;
he is my fortress, I will not be shaken.
My salvation and my honor depend on God;
he is my mighty rock, my refuge.
Trust in him at all times, O people;
pour out your hearts to him,
for God is our refuge.

Psalm *62:5-8*

The God Who Responds

From Genesis to Malachi we have ample proof of prayer being fully answered by God. No sincere saint was sent away empty. No petition in submission to the divine will failed of an appropriate answer.

Herbert Lockyer

He answered their prayers, because they trusted in him.

1 Chronicles *5:20*

To answer prayer is God's universal rule. God's word does not say, "Call unto me, and you will thereby be trained into the happy art of knowing how to be denied. Ask, and you will learn sweet patience by getting nothing." Far from it. But it is definite, clear and positive: "Ask, and it shall be given unto you."

E. M. Bounds

The Bible says that God is anxious to answer our prayers, that He's *eager* to do so, that He really wants to grant our requests. If we ask God for something that's good and God sees that it's good for us, He will give it to us.

David Jeremiah

Jesus said, "Which of you, if his son asks for bread, will give him a stone? Or if he asks for a fish, will give him a snake? If you, then, though you are evil, know how to give good gifts to your children, how much more will your Father in heaven give good gifts to those who ask him!"

Matthew *7:9-11*

This is the confidence we have in approaching God: that if we ask anything according to his will, he hears us.

1 John *5:14*

I will make rivers flow on barren heights,
and springs within the valleys.
I will turn the desert into pools of water,
and the parched ground into springs.

Isaiah *41:18*

The God Who Hears

O you who hear prayer,
to you all men will come.

Psalm *65:2*

Let this be understood above all: the power of prayer is
not in us, that we speak. It is in God, that he listens!

Walter Wangerin

God does not stand afar off as I struggle to speak. He
cares enough to listen with more than casual attention.
He "translates" my scrubby words and hears what is
truly inside. He hears my sighs and uncertain gropings
as fine prose.

Timothy Jones

Before they call I will answer;
while they are still speaking I will hear.

Isaiah *65:24*

A Swift Salvation

Jesus made the disciples get into the boat and go on ahead of him to the other side, while he dismissed the crowd.... When evening came, the boat was already a considerable distance from land, buffeted by the waves because the wind was against it. During the fourth watch of the night Jesus went out to them, walking on the lake. When the disciples saw him walking on the lake, they were terrified. "It's a ghost," they said, and cried out in fear. But Jesus immediately said to them:

"Take courage! It is I. Don't be afraid."

"Lord, if it's you," Peter replied, "tell me to come to you on the water."

"Come," he said. Then Peter got down out of the boat, walked on the water and came toward Jesus. But when he saw the wind, he was afraid and, beginning to sink, cried out, "Lord, save me!" Immediately Jesus reached out his hand and caught him. "You of little faith," he said, "why did you doubt?"

And when they climbed into the boat, the wind died down. Then those who were in the boat worshiped him, saying, "Truly you are the Son of God."

Matthew *14:22, 23–33*

How many seconds lie between a man's beginning to
sink and his sinking? A single second or less,
I suppose. How swift, then, was the movement of love!
And as He was, so He is.

Amy Carmichael

So do not fear, for I am with you;
do not be dismayed, for I am your God.
I will strengthen you and help you;
I will uphold you with my righteous right hand.

Isaiah *41:10*

My soul clings to you;
your right hand upholds me.

Psalm *63:8*

God's Timing

I have learned that God's timing is not my timing in the big and little things about which I pray. Sometimes God keeps me persisting in prayer, becoming more fervent in my wrestling with Him, through days, months, even years. I just wait for His answer to come—when He decides it is time to send it. But He always answers.

Evelyn Christenson

"My thoughts are not your thoughts,
neither are your ways my ways," declares the LORD.
"As the heavens are higher than the earth,
so are my ways higher than your ways
and my thoughts than your thoughts."

Isaiah 55:8-9

Lord Jesus, I know that the seasons come and go in majestic sequence. The earth rotates on its axis in a predetermined rhythm. No prayers of mine could change any of this. I know that Your ways are not my ways; Your timing is not my timing. But Lord, how do I, so earthbound, come to terms with the pace of eternity?

Catherine Marshall

I will proclaim the name of the LORD.
Oh, praise the greatness of our God!
He is the Rock, his works are perfect,
and all his ways are just.
A faithful God who does no wrong,
upright and just is he.

Deuteronomy *32:3-4*

When God doesn't show up when you think He
should, don't get discouraged. Many times I have
prayed believing that my prayer was part of God's perfect will, yet He didn't move as quickly as I wanted
Him to. One time I had to wait sixteen years for Him
to answer. But when He did, it was the right answer at
the right time. While I was waiting on Him, I wondered what was happening. Sometimes I asked if He
really heard me. Was I praying right? What else could
I do? But deep within He assured me that He would
see me through. He'll do the same for you.

Thelma Wells

If the ships of prayer do not come home speedily, it is
because they are more heavily freighted with blessing.

Charles Spurgeon

Never Too Late

Now a man named Lazarus was sick. He was from
Bethany, the village of Mary and her sister Martha. . . .
The sisters sent word to Jesus, "Lord, the one you love
is sick.". . . Jesus loved Martha and her sister and
Lazarus. Yet when he heard that Lazarus was sick, he
stayed where he was two more days. . . .

On his arrival, Jesus found that Lazarus had
already been in the tomb for four days. . . . When
Martha heard that Jesus was coming, she went out to
meet him, but Mary stayed at home. "Lord," Martha
said to Jesus, "if you had been here, my brother would
not have died. But I know that even now God will
give you whatever you ask." Jesus said to her, "Your
brother will rise again.". . .

Jesus came to the tomb. It was a cave with a stone
laid across the entrance.

"Take away the stone," he said. . . . When he had
said this, Jesus called in a loud voice, "Lazarus, come
out!" The dead man came out, his hands and feet
wrapped with strips of linen, and a cloth around his
face. Jesus said to them, "Take off the grave clothes
and let him go."

John 11:1, 3, 5–6, 17, 20–23, 38–39, 43–44

Watching and Waiting

Waiting is vigilance plus expectation;
it is wide awake to God.

Eugene H. Peterson

All three of [Jesus'] commands are present imperatives:
"Keep on asking, *keep on* seeking, *keep on* knocking."
Don't ever stop asking, don't ever stop seeking, don't
ever stop knocking. Just keep at it. Keep bringing your
prayers to God. God wants to teach us through persis-
tent praying to wait on Him and to watch. While we're
praying and waiting for God to answer our prayers, do
you know what He's doing? He's working on us, con-
forming us more and more to the image of Christ. And
when we're ready, the answer will surely come.

David Jeremiah

But as for me, I watch in hope for the LORD,
I wait for God my Savior;
my God will hear me.
Do not gloat over me, my enemy!
Though I have fallen, I will rise.
Though I sit in darkness,
the LORD will be my light.

Micah 7:7-8

God Is Able

God is alive and active, able to do what we ask. God
hears and answers prayer, as our true friend. God is
also able to do what we imagine. He reads our
thoughts and can interpret the thoughts and feelings
we cannot express as we cry out to him in distress.
God is able to do all that we ask or think. He is the
King of kings and Lord of lords. He knows everything
and can complete the work he started in us.

James Houston

Being confident of this, that he who began a good
work in you will carry it on to completion until the
day of Christ Jesus.

Philippians 1:6

For the LORD is a God of justice.
Blessed are all who wait for him!

Isaiah 30:18

Lift your eyes and look to the heavens:
Who created all these?
He who brings out the starry host one by one,
and calls them each by name.
Because of his great power and mighty strength,
not one of them is missing.

Why do you say, O Jacob,
and complain, O Israel,
"My way is hidden from the LORD;
my cause is disregarded by my God"?
Do you not know?
Have you not heard?
The LORD is the everlasting God,
the Creator of the ends of the earth.
He will not grow tired or weary,
and his understanding no one can fathom.
He gives strength to the weary
and increases the power of the weak.
Even youths grow tired and weary,
and young men stumble and fall;
but those who hope in the LORD
will renew their strength.
They will soar on wings like eagles;
they will run and not grow weary,
they will walk and not be faint.

Isaiah *40:26-31*

The God Who Delivers

God is joy spilling over. This is where his mercy comes from. The full tank of love he enjoys is splashing out over heaven's walls. He swims in elation and is driven to share it with us. Why? Simply, as he put it, "so that my joy may be in you:" (John 15:11).

Joni Eareckson Tada

That we want to pray suggests that there is someone waiting for us to speak, waiting to listen.

Timothy Jones

You are forgiving and good, O LORD,
abounding in love to all who call to you.
Hear my prayer, O LORD;
listen to my cry for mercy.
In the day of my trouble I will call to you,
for you will answer me.

Psalm *86:5–7*

Lord, to whom shall we go? You have the words of eternal life. We believe and know that you are the Holy One of God.

John *6:68–69*

Call upon me in the day of trouble;
I will deliver you, and you will honor me.

Psalm *50:15*

God has given His promise that when we call He will
deliver. He doesn't say, "I may deliver," "I will try to
deliver," "Perhaps I will deliver," "I will deliver if I feel
like it," or "If I'm not too busy I will deliver," but "I
WILL deliver." He who promised to deliver, has the
power to do it.

Millie Stamm

"Because he loves me," says the LORD, "I will rescue
him;
I will protect him, for he acknowledges my name.
He will call upon me, and I will answer him;
I will be with him in trouble,
I will deliver him and honor him."

Psalm *91:14–15*

The one who calls you is faithful and he will do it.

1 Thessalonians *5:24*

The Lord Is My Refuge

The LORD is my light and my salvation—
whom shall I fear?
The LORD is the stronghold of my life—
of whom shall I be afraid?
When evil men advance against me
to devour my flesh,
when my enemies and my foes attack me,
they will stumble and fall.
Though an army besiege me,
my heart will not fear;
though war break out against me,
even then will I be confident. . . .

For in the day of trouble
he will keep me safe in his dwelling;
he will hide me in the shelter of his tabernacle
and set me high upon a rock.
Then my head will be exalted
above the enemies who surround me;
at his tabernacle will I sacrifice with shouts of joy;
I will sing and make music to the LORD. . . .

I am still confident of this:
I will see the goodness of the LORD
in the land of the living.
Wait for the LORD;
be strong and take heart
and wait for the LORD.

Psalm *27:1-3, 5-6, 13-14*

Look to my right and see;
no one is concerned for me.
I have no refuge;
no one cares for my life.

Psalm *142:4*

Trouble does its best work when it drives us to God.
The discovery that other people cannot or will not help
us is not a disaster if, at the same time, it shows us that
God both can and will help. That we are abandoned by
others is not the last straw so much as the first step to
the realization that God is our help and salvation.

*In the empty places in my life, devastated by broken
promises and vacated by faithless companions, come, Holy
Spirit, as Companion and Comforter. I will use my times
of trouble to receive the help that only you can give.*
Amen.

Eugene H. Peterson

Though my father and mother forsake me,
the LORD will receive me.

Psalm *27:10*

Just Pray

Cares and worries are manifold; therefore let your prayers be manifold. Turn everything that is a care into a prayer. Let your cares be the raw material of your prayers. As the alchemist hoped to turn dross into gold, you have the power to actually turn what naturally would have been a care into a spiritual treasure in the form of a prayer. Baptize every anxiety into the name of the Father, the Son, and the Holy Spirit, and so make it into a blessing.

Charles Spurgeon

Do not be anxious about anything, but in everything, by prayer and petition, with thanksgiving, present your requests to God. And the peace of God, which transcends all understanding, will guard your hearts and your minds in Christ Jesus. Cast your cares on the LORD and he will sustain you; he will never let the righteous fall. For God is greater than our hearts, and he knows everything.

Philippians *4:6-7*; Psalm *55:22*; 1 John *3:20*

Jesus taught us to pray for daily bread. Have you ever noticed that children ask for lunch in utter confidence that it will be provided? They have no need to stash away today's sandwiches for fear none will be available tomorrow. As far as they are concerned, there is an endless supply of sandwiches.

Richard J. Foster

The
Prayerful
Heart

Listening from the Heart

Holy moments come to us daily if we will ask for eyes to see. We can't always withdraw to quiet hillsides to pray, but Christ will meet with us in the quiet places of our hearts.

Sheila Walsh

Talking to God is more art than science, more a relationship than a set of techniques. It asks us to listen to our hearts as much as to our heads. It involves our deepest selves and our most everyday moments.

Timothy Jones

Life is not ultimately problem but mystery. To listen to its depths is finally to find oneself on one's knees.

Wendy M. Wright

God speaks to us. In love he responds. He talks back, answers, makes himself known, makes his being known, makes his being and his intentions real unto us so that we who call may meet and recognize the listener to our call; so that we who love may know the object of our loving.

Except we wait for that, we are merely using God, reducing the Almighty to a candy machine whose only purpose is to respond when we punch its buttons, satisfying the hungers we define. But God is alive. He participates in conversation. His yearning is to be heard as well as to hear, to lead, to explain, to console, to solve and resolve not only our problems but our very *selves*, to satisfy not only the petty hungers we can name, but the deeper hungers only a Holy Father can identify.

Walter Wangerin

Be Still

Be still, and know that I am God;
I will be exalted among the nations,
I will be exalted in the earth.

Psalm *46:10*

The world says, "Be active; be busy; be industrious."
But God says, "BE STILL; be quiet; don't rush." This
is not just a cessation of activities, but a quietness of
heart and spirit in which we are aware of His presence.
In the center of our soul is a place where God dwells,
and where, if we enter and close out every other
sound, He will speak to us.

Millie Stamm

We will find no rest for our heart or spirit as long as
we seek it in insignificant things which cannot satisfy
us, rather than in God who is omnipotent, omni-
scient, and beneficent. He is our true repose.

Julian of Norwich

Delight yourself in the LORD
and he will give you the desires of your heart.

Commit your way to the LORD;
trust in him and he will do this:
He will make your righteousness shine like the dawn,
the justice of your cause like the noonday sun.

Be still before the LORD and wait patiently for him;
do not fret when men succeed in their ways,
when they carry out their wicked schemes. . . .

If the LORD delights in a man's way,
he makes his steps firm;
though he stumble, he will not fall,
for the LORD upholds him with his hand.

I was young and now I am old,
yet I have never seen the righteous forsaken
or their children begging bread.
They are always generous and lend freely;
their children will be blessed.

Psalm *37:4-7, 23-26*

Intimate Union

The union with the Son of God is a life union. We are indeed one with Him. Our prayer ascends as His prayer. It is because we abide in Him that we can ask what we will, and it is given to us.

Andrew Murray

Prayer is nothing else than being on terms of friendship with God. It is frequently conversing in secret with Him Who loves us.

St. Teresa of Avila

In the Christian life it is of more than passing significance to observe that those who are the most serene, most confident, and most able to cope with life's complexities often are those who rise early each day to feed on God's Word. It is in the quiet, early hours of the morning that they are led beside the quiet, still waters where they imbibe the very life of Christ for the day. This is much more than mere figure of speech. It is practical reality. The biographies of the great men and women of God repeatedly point out how the secret of the success in their spiritual life was attributed to the "quiet time" of each morning. There, alone, still, waiting for the Master's voice, one is led gently to the place where, as the old hymn puts it, "The still dews of His Spirit can be dropped into my life and soul."

W. Phillip Keller

Remain in me, and I will remain in you. No branch can bear fruit by itself; it must remain in the vine. Neither can you bear fruit unless you remain in me. I am the vine; you are the branches. If a man remains in me and I in him, he will bear much fruit; apart from me you can do nothing. If anyone does not remain in me, he is like a branch that is thrown away and withers; such branches are picked up, thrown into the fire and burned. If you remain in me and my words remain in you, ask whatever you wish, and it will be given you. This is to my Father's glory, that you bear much fruit, showing yourselves to be my disciples. As the Father has loved me, so have I loved you. Now remain in my love. If you obey my commands, you will remain in my love, just as I have obeyed my Father's commands and remain in his love. I have told you this so that my joy may be in you and that your joy may be complete.

John 15:4-11

Beyond Words

Prayer is infinitely more than simply the use of words in addressing the Heavenly Father. Prayer is really an attitude of the heart.

Don Sanford

While most of us would quickly define prayer as something expressed in words, I see it more fundamentally as our being in God's presence. Sometimes words are eminently appropriate. But sometimes they get in the way. And often they simply don't matter. The important thing is to stand before God without our constant chatter, ready to be in heartfelt relationship with him. Where our whole selves are engaged in relationship with God, there prayer will be, even if words are not used.

Timothy Jones

The Sweetest Presence

Happy is he who opens his heart to you, good Jesus, for you enter and rest there. You bring the midday of heavenly light to the troubled breast, calming every emotion of the heart with the rays of divine peace. You make a bed within the soul with fragrant spiritual flowers, and you lie upon it, so that the soul is filled with the knowledge of you and the joy of your sweetness.

Aelred of Rievaulx

Dearest Child,

Let prayer become the breath of your spirit. Let it be the beating of your heart. Be aware of my presence at all times. Come simply before me without anxiety and let the roots of your spirit go deep. Remain in a thankful awareness of my nearness all day as you work at the gentle occupation of being my child. And a deep, sweet peace will stand guard over your thoughts and your emotions as you live and move and have your being in me. That is when your heart will discover that to live a whole day in the awareness of my presence is the loveliest prayer of all!

Be at home in me,
Abba
Claire Cloninger

Listen!

Hearing or listening is a good metaphor for prayer.
The good pray-er is above all a good listener. Prayer is
dialogue; it is a personal encounter in love. When we
communicate with someone we care about, we speak
and we listen. But even our speaking is responsive:
What we say depends upon what the other person has
said to us. Otherwise we don't have real dialogue, but
rather two monologues running along side by side.

Thomas S. Green, S.J.

Prayer is both speaking *and* listening. As I use an
economy of words I redeem time to listen, and in so
doing, I make prayer the dialogue it was intended to
be. I do not pray to hear myself speak; rather, I pray in
order that I may hear God speak.

Steve Harper

To listen deeply; to listen with a tender, yielding heart;
to listen adventurously enough to be utterly surprised
at what we hear; this we all need to be able to do. We
all need, in one way or another, at one time or another, to enter the desert and listen there mutely, intently
for God.

Wendy M. Wright

"Speak, Lord..."

The boy Samuel ministered before the LORD under Eli. In those days the word of the LORD was rare; there were not many visions.

One night Eli, whose eyes were becoming so weak that he could barely see, was lying down in his usual place. The lamp of God had not yet gone out, and Samuel was lying down in the temple of the LORD, where the ark of God was.

Then the LORD called Samuel. Samuel answered, "Here I am." And he ran to Eli and said, "Here I am; you called me." But Eli said, "I did not call; go back and lie down." So he went and lay down.

Again the LORD called, "Samuel!" And Samuel got up and went to Eli and said, "Here I am; you called me."

"My son," Eli said, "I did not call; go back and lie down."

Now Samuel did not yet know the LORD: The word of the LORD had not yet been revealed to him. The LORD called Samuel a third time, and Samuel got up and went to Eli and said, "Here I am; you called me."

Then Eli realized that the LORD was calling the boy. So Eli told Samuel, "Go and lie down, and if he calls you, say, 'Speak, LORD, for your servant is listening.'" So Samuel went and lay down in his place.

The LORD came and stood there, calling as at the other times, "Samuel! Samuel!" Then Samuel said, "Speak, for your servant is listening." And the LORD said to Samuel: "See, I am about to do something in Israel that will make the ears of everyone who hears of it tingle."

1 Samuel *3:1-11*

The Voice We Can Trust

The LORD would speak to Moses face to face, as a man speaks with his friend.

Exodus *33:11*

I believe God talks to us. Have I ever heard God speak to me in an audible voice? No.
Sometimes He speaks to me through Scripture.
Sometimes He speaks to me
- through the words of a song.
- through a reading or a sermon.
- through a quote of advice or admonition.
- through the honesty of a child.
- from a billboard or a bumper sticker.
- through a conversation with a family member or friend.

He always tells me things that are in line with His Holy Word.
He does not always give me all the details.
His information is always correct.
When I follow His directions, I will make no mistakes.
He brings to pass everything He says.
I am amazed and humbled to realize that an awesome, omnipotent, sovereign God would want to communicate with me. But that's one of the reasons He created us: He wants us to have fellowship with Him. People have tried to explain how to hear the voice of God. In my opinion, nobody has been able to describe it fully. I believe God's sheep know the Shepherd's voice by faith.

Thelma Wells

Jesus said, "The man who enters by the gate is the shepherd of his sheep. The watchman opens the gate for him, and the sheep listen to his voice. He calls his own sheep by name and leads them out. When he has brought out all his own, he goes on ahead of them, and his sheep follow him because they know his voice.". . .

"I am the good shepherd; I know my sheep and my sheep know me—just as the Father knows me and I know the Father—and I lay down my life for the sheep."

"My sheep listen to my voice; I know them, and they follow me. I give them eternal life, and they shall never perish; no one can snatch them out of my hand. My Father, who has given them to me, is greater than all; no one can snatch them out of my Father's hand. I and the Father are one."

John *10:2-4, 14-15, 27-30*

Lord, teach me to listen. The times are noisy and my ears are weary with the thousand raucous sounds which continuously assualt them. Give me the spirit of the boy Samuel when he said to Thee, "Speak, for thy servant heareth." Let me hear Thee speaking in my heart. Let me get used to the sound of Thy voice, that its tones may be familiar when the sounds of earth die away and the only sound will be the music of Thy speaking. Amen.

A. W. Tozer

Filled to Overflowing

On the last and greatest day of the Feast, Jesus stood and said in a loud voice, "If anyone is thirsty, let him come to me and drink. Whoever believes in me, as the Scripture has said, streams of living water will flow from within him." By this he meant the Spirit, whom those who believed in him were later to receive.

John 7:37-39

If I am to be fit and healthy and strong in body I must drink fresh, clean, pure water day after day. If I am to be strong, buoyant, and serene in spirit I must drink anew of Christ's Spirit and life day after day. Then, and only then, can there flow from my own innermost being rivers of His living water to refresh others. We are but the channels through which He can pour the power and refreshment of His own life. In stillness we repose in Him, open to His presence, allowing Him to fill us constantly!

W. Phillip Keller

[Christ] does not think of prayer as a means of getting blessing for ourselves, but as one of the chief channels of influence by which the blessings of Christ's redemption are dispensed to the world.

Andrew Murray

The Abiding Heart

My Child,

Come into my presence today. Take refuge in me and experience my goodness. Look to me in every situation, and your face will be radiant. When your heart is empty and aching, you will find fullness and healing in me. When your spirit is brimming with joy, I will be there to share it with you. Whether the future looks bright and hopeful or the way ahead looks impassable, whether your dreams are as clear as glass or as murky as a mud puddle, see me here. Know my nearness. Bring all to me every trial and every triumph, every hope and every fear, every burden and every blessing. Live every moment in my presence.

Your loving Abba,
God

Claire Cloninger

Come Lord Jesus, and abide in my heart. How grateful I am to realize that the answer to my prayer does not depend on me at all. As I quietly abide in You and let Your life flow into me, what freedom it is to know that the Father does not see my threadbare patience or insufficient trust, rather only Your patience, Lord, and Your confidence that the Father has everything in hand.

In Your faith I thank You right now for a more glorious answer to my prayer than I can imagine. *Amen.*

Catherine Marshall

So
Many
Ways to
Pray

🍁

Anytime Prayers

Effective prayer is not measured by its length but by its depth. It doesn't require a Ph.D.—it only requires a willingness to share your thoughts with God.

Joni Eareckson Tada

"BE STILL," my soul, for just as thou art still,
Can God reveal Himself to thee; until
Through thee His love and light and life can freely flow;
In stillness God can work through thee and reach
The souls around thee. He then through thee can teach
His lessons, and His power in weakness show.

Selected

Our prayer might be as minuscule as a sigh to express our pain. Or it might be an ephemeral cloud-puff of a thought just before we plunge into a joyful moment. When that sigh or that half-formed thought is sent in God's direction, he is there to clasp it in his hands.

Janet Kobobel Grant

We are mystics of the ordinary life. I may sense God's presence while out for a morning run, driving to my office, or simply waiting in line at a supermarket checkout aisle. We will sense him in a moment of profound stillness in a sanctuary, at a cresting of a hill on a mountain drive that takes our breath away, or during a dawning awareness that unseen arms uphold us during a harrowing chapter in our lives. The conviction will come that around me, above me, is Someone. I realize, *I am not alone.* And I pray.

Timothy Jones

Praying is the sound God's family makes when we are in right relationship with God. The spectrum of that sound includes praise, thanksgiving, confession, petition, intercession, worship, the wonderful hubbub of earnest talking and listening between children and a heavenly Father.

David and Heather Kopp

Telegraph Prayers

Some brethren pray by the yard, but true prayer is measured by weight—not by length. A single groan before God may have more fullness of prayer in it than a fine oration of great length.

Charles Spurgeon

Our loving Lord is not just present, but nearer than thought can imagine—so near that a whisper can reach Him. You know the story of the man who had a quick temper and had no time to go away and pray for help. His habit was to send up a little telegraph prayer— "Thy sweetness, Lord!"—and sweetness came. Do you need courage? "Thy courage, Lord!" Patience? "Thy patience, Lord!" Love? "Thy love, Lord!" A quiet mind? "Thy quietness, Lord!"

Shall we practice this swift and simple way of prayer more and more? If we do, our Very Present Help will not disappoint us. For Thou, Lord, hast never failed them that seek Thee.

Amy Carmichael

"Help!" is prayer in fine form, jangled exclamation and all.

Timothy Jones

The Lord is my peace. I shall not live in anxiety. He puts me under his wing of comfort and calms my spirit within me. He takes all my anxieties on Himself and helps me to focus on Him. Yes, though I walk through a time of grave uncertainties and fierce anxieties, I will not fret—for You are my peace. Your Word and Your presence calm me now. You hold my uncertainties in the palm of Your hand. You soothe my anxious mind—You smooth my wrinkled brow. Surely serenity and trust in You shall fill me all the days of my life. And I shall keep my mind stayed on You forever.

Judy Booth

A Very Present Help

God is our refuge and strength,
A very present help in trouble.
Therefore we will not fear, though the earth should
change,
And though the mountains slip into the heart of the sea;
Though its waters roar and foam,
Though the mountains quake at its swelling pride.

There is a river whose streams make glad the city of
God,
The holy dwelling places of the Most High.
God is in the midst of her, she will not be moved;
God will help her when morning dawns.
The nations made an uproar, the kingdoms tottered;
He raised His voice, the earth melted.
The LORD of hosts is with us;
The God of Jacob is our stronghold.

Come, behold the works of the LORD,
Who has wrought desolations in the earth.
He makes wars to cease to the end of the earth;
He breaks the bow and cuts the spear in two;
He burns the chariots with fire.
"Cease striving and know that I am God;
I will be exalted among the nations,
I will be exalted in the earth."
The LORD of hosts is with us;
the God of Jacob is our stronghold.

Psalm *46:1–11*, NASB

Prayers of the Moment

In the month of Nisan in the twentieth year of King Artaxerxes, when wine was brought for him, I took the wine and gave it to the king. I had not been sad in his presence before; so the king asked me, "Why does your face look so sad when you are not ill? This can be nothing but sadness of heart."

I was very much afraid, but I said to the king, "May the king live forever! Why should my face not look sad when the city where my fathers are buried lies in ruins, and its gates have been destroyed by fire?"

The king said to me, "What is it you want?" Then I prayed to the God of heaven, and I answered the king, "If it pleases the king and if your servant has found favor in his sight, let him send me to the city in Judah where my fathers are buried so that I can rebuild it."

Then the king, with the queen sitting beside him, asked me, "How long will your journey take, and when will you get back?" It pleased the king to send me; so I set a time.

Nehemiah 2:1-6

King Artaxerxes' question of what Nehemiah wishes to do for Jerusalem is followed by an immediate prayer for help. This was not the prayer that stands knocking at mercy's door, but it was the concentration of many knocks in one. It was introduced between the king's question and Nehemiah's answer. Probably the interval was not long enough to be noticed, but it was long enough for God to notice it—long enough for Nehemiah to have sought and obtained guidance from God as to how to answer the king. Nehemiah, being "very much afraid" at the moment, offered his prayer like an electric flash, like the winking of an eye. It was done intuitively, yet done it was, and it proved to be a prayer that prevailed with God.

Never underestimate the value of a prayer of the moment. Nehemiah's prayer—a little bit of a prayer pushed in sideways between a question and an answer, a mere fragment of devotion—was never erased from these words of biblical history.

Charles Spurgeon

The Cry of Emptiness

O LORD, hear my prayer,
listen to my cry for mercy;
in your faithfulness and righteousness
come to my relief. . . .

I spread out my hands to you;
my soul thirsts for you like a parched land.
Answer me quickly, O LORD;
my spirit fails.
Do not hide your face from me
or I will be like those who go down to the pit.

Psalm *143:1, 6–7*

Prayer is a cry from the bare spot in our lives, from the
empty space, from the part of us that is missing. It is
the wounded part seeking to be healed, the missing
part seeking to be found, the now-dry clay of the
sculpture seeking the hands that first touched it, first
caressed it, first loved it.

Ken Gire

Every request I make of God is a message telling of my
neediness, of my trust in God, of my willing dependence and openness to receive. My requests are often
foolish, as I am, but God is well able to cope.

Michael Casey

Blessed are those who hunger and thirst for righteousness, for they will be filled.

Matthew *5:6*

I need you, O God. I cannot sustain meaning and purpose by myself. I don't have within me the stuff to make life whole. I run out of resources. I run out of strength. In my emptiness I wait for your fullness. Keep me always conscious, Father, of my need and your salvation, of the perils of sin and the mercies of deliverance, of my empty hands and your bountiful grace, through Jesus Christ. *Amen.*
Eugene H. Peterson

Breathe on me, Breath of God,
Fill me with life anew,
That I may love what Thou dost love,
And do what Thou wouldst do.

Breathe on me, Breath of God,
Till I am wholly Thine,
Till all this earthly part of me
Glows with Thy fire divine.
Edwin Hatch

The Prayer of Petition

Be pleased, O LORD, to save me;
O LORD, come quickly to help me.
May all who seek to take my life
be put to shame and confusion;
may all who desire my ruin
be turned back in disgrace. . . .

Yet I am poor and needy;
may the Lord think of me.
You are my help and my deliverer;
O my God, do not delay.

Psalm *40:13–14, 17*

Blessed are all thy Saints, O God and King, who have
travelled over the tempestuous sea of this mortal life,
and have made the harbour of peace and felicity. Watch
over us who are still in our dangerous voyage; and
remember such as lie exposed to the rough storms of
trouble and temptations. Frail is our vessel, and the
ocean is wide; but as in thy mercy thou has set our
course, so steer the vessel of our life toward the everlasting shore of peace, and bring us at length to the quiet
haven of our heart's desire, where thou, O our God, are
blessed, and livest and reignest for ever and ever.

St. Augustine

Do you know why the mighty God of the universe chooses to answer prayer? It is because his children ask. God delights in our asking. He is pleased at our asking. His heart is warmed by our asking.

Richard J. Foster

Petitionary prayer reminds us that God is not a God far off. He has come very close to us and is intimately involved in all the concerns of our human life. He is doing things in this world of ours. Of course he does not interfere wantonly and at random with the freedom and independence he has given to us nor with the regularity of his creation; he does not act in a way that would contradict the gentleness and delicacy of his rule. But that does not mean that he is little more than an absentee landlord. Prayer of petition is always an act of faith in this immediacy of God's presence.

Simon Tugwell

The Prayer of Anguish

I cry aloud to the LORD;
I lift up my voice to the LORD for mercy.
I pour out my complaint before him;
before him I tell my trouble.

Psalm 142:1–2

I loathe my very life;
therefore I will give free rein to my complaint
and speak out in the bitterness of my soul.

Job 10:1

My heart is in anguish within me;
the terrors of death assail me.
Fear and trembling have beset me;
horror has overwhelmed me.
I said, "Oh, that I had the wings of a dove!
I would fly away and be at rest—
I would flee far away
and stay in the desert;
I would hurry to my place of shelter,
far from the tempest and storm."

Psalm 55:4–8

We do not have to "dress up," either inwardly or out-
wardly, when we come to God in prayer. We do not
have to hide our anger, suppress our distress, or mask
our irritability. It is all right to complain to God.

Eugene H. Peterson

We may babble or roar or weep or sigh or put our
foreheads against an old stone wall and wail.
Walter Wangerin

Our prayers represent not just what we say but who
we are, with all our complex longings and feelings. To
be close to someone, even when that someone is God,
will inevitably run us through a gamut of emotions. To
think prayer should be a monochrome pattern is to
rob it of its power. A wide and sometimes wild range
of feelings accompanies a walk with God.

Many of the prayers in the Bible are rough-edged and
unrefined to an astonishing degree. They sometimes
make us wince. But seeing such raw intensity reminds
me that I can blurt out my words in panic or in pain,
not just when I am feeling holy. God wants *me*. I do
not put on airs or try to give myself a spiritual
makeover to talk to God.
Timothy Jones

The Prayer of Contrition

Have mercy on me, O God,
according to your unfailing love;
according to your great compassion
blot out my transgressions.
Wash away all my iniquity
and cleanse me from my sin.

For I know my transgressions,
and my sin is always before me.
Against you, you only, have I sinned
and done what is evil in your sight,
so that you are proved right when you speak
and justified when you judge.
Surely I was sinful at birth,
sinful from the time my mother conceived me.
Surely you desire truth in the inner parts;
you teach me wisdom in the inmost place.

Cleanse me with hyssop, and I will be clean;
wash me, and I will be whiter than snow.
Let me hear joy and gladness;
let the bones you have crushed rejoice.
Hide your face from my sins
and blot out all my iniquity.

Create in me a pure heart, O God,
and renew a steadfast spirit within me.
Do not cast me from your presence
or take your Holy Spirit from me.
Restore to me the joy of your salvation
and grant me a willing spirit, to sustain me.

Then I will teach transgressors your ways,
and sinners will turn back to you.
Save me from bloodguilt, O God,
the God who saves me,
and my tongue will sing of your righteousness.
O LORD, open my lips,
and my mouth will declare your praise.
You do not delight in sacrifice, or I would bring it;
you do not take pleasure in burnt offerings.
The sacrifices of God are a broken spirit;
a broken and contrite heart,
O God, you will not despise.

In your good pleasure make Zion prosper;
build up the walls of Jerusalem.
Then there will be righteous sacrifices,
whole burnt offerings to delight you;
then bulls will be offered on your altar.

Psalm *51*

Gracious Father—high King of heaven, yet my Father!—
You are seated in the throne room of the universe on a
throne of grace, a throne of favor for the undeserving.
What a privilege it is to come to your throne unafraid,
with utter freedom and confidence, assured of Your glad
welcome. To know that I'll find mercy for my failures and
grace for my every need! What good news that I don't need
to be almost perfect to come boldly into Your presence! Your
mercy lets me come with my mistakes, my sins, my needs.
Thank You that You are always ready to forgive, always
eager to hear my voice and answer my prayers.

Warren and Ruth Myers

Tender Mercies

Awareness of sin serves as a great generator of prayer. To go to prayer aware of the shabbiness of my life is a great blessing. I can approach God as the great Healer of life's wounds, reveal myself in truth, and receive help. If I avoid the issue by keeping up a barrage of words and holy thoughts, I end up exhausted.... My failures, I must learn, do not separate me from God. What causes the breach is an unwillingness to bring my failures into God's presence. The greater failure is not realizing that God's attitude to my sin is pity, not blame.

Michael Casey

If we could remember that the divine mercy is not a temporary mood but an attribute of God's eternal being, we would no longer fear that it will someday cease to be. Nothing that has occurred or will occur in heaven or earth or hell can change the tender mercies of our God. Forever His mercy stands, a boundless, over-whelming immensity of divine pity and compassion.

A. W. Tozer

Contrition before God is not a fearful cowering of the kind we observe in an abused animal, but an honest openness that is confident of mercy.

Eugene H. Peterson

You want to wash away your sins; there is a river of grace to wash in. You want grace to refresh your souls; He has floods to pour upon the dry ground. Ho! you leviathan sinners, here is an ocean of mercy for you to swim in. Ho! you elephantine sinners, here is an ark large enough to hold you and float you above the waters of the deluge! You whose sins of pride reach up to heaven and whose feet of lust are plunged into the mire of hell, the sacred hiding place is large enough to hide even you. The Lord is great in mercy.

Charles Spurgeon

The birds have their nests and the foxes have their holes. But you were homeless, Lord Jesus, with nowhere to rest your head. And yet you were a hiding-place where the sinner could flee. Today you are such a hiding-place, and I flee to you. I hide myself under your wings, and your wings cover the multitude of my sins.

Søren Kierkegaard

Always in Touch

[To pray] *always* means that the soul that has come into intimate contact with God in the silence of the prayer chamber is never out of conscious touch with the Father; that the heart is always going out to Him in loving communion; and that the moment the mind is released from the task upon which it is engaged, it returns as naturally to God as the bird does to its nest.

E. M. Bounds

Precious Child,

Prayer is to the spirit what breathing is to the body. It is a natural and essential grace that feeds the spirit as oxygen feeds the body. When should you pray? At all times! Begin to think of prayer as a ceaseless flow of life in the hearts of those who love me. It is a moment-by-moment dialogue between Father and child. But it is so much more than forming ideas and sentences. Prayer is turning every thought to me. It is inviting me to be part of every idea and decision. I already know your unspoken thoughts, so direct those thoughts to me all day long, and you will be praying continually.

Lovingly,
Abba

Claire Cloninger

Coming LORD!

My Child,

Don't try to hide your failure from me. Don't try to resolve your conflicts on your own before you come to me. That is like trying to clean up your house for the housekeeper! Instead, run into my presence with the confidence of a beloved child, for that is who you are to me. Bring me your sins and failures. Lay them on my altar and confess them. Don't you know that I see you as you are and yet I love you? Because of what my Son, Jesus, has done for you there is mercy waiting. Because of him, whatever you confess I will forgive, and whatever you have failed in I will redeem. Don't wait until you are better. This life of prayer is a "come-as-you-are" affair.

So, come!
Abba

Claire Cloninger

Son of God, perform a miracle for me: change my heart. You, whose crimson blood redeems mankind, whiten my heart.
It is you who makes the sun bright and the ice sparkle; you who makes the rivers flow and the salmon leap.
Your skilled hand makes the nut tree blossom, and the corn turn golden; your spirit composes the songs of the birds and the buzz of the bees.
Your creation is a million wondrous miracles, beautiful to behold. I ask of you just one more miracle: beautify my soul.

Celtic Prayer

The Prayer of Intercession

God, our Father, there are no two of us with the same
need. You know our needs. Specifically bless those who
are in the middle of some specially difficult time:
Those who have some specially difficult task to face;
Those who have some specially difficult problem to solve;
Those who have some specially difficult decision to make;
Those who have some specially difficult temptation to resist;
Those who have some specially baffling doubt through
which to think their way.
Speak to those who are
Evading some decision;
Shirking some task;
Putting off some duty;
Playing with fire;
Wasting their time;
Throwing away their opportunities.
Speak to those who are successful, that they may be kept
from all pride and self-conceit; speak to those who are too
self-confident, that they may not be riding for a fall; speak
to those who are too sure that they are right and too sure
that everyone else is wrong, that they may be kept from
intolerance. Help those who are shy. Remember those
who are in disgrace, and keep them from despair.

William Barclay

Praying for other people is perhaps the most powerful, loving, influential relational activity we can perform for someone.

Dudley J. Delffs

In 1963 many mine disasters occurred around the world. Over and over again came the good news that a hole was being bored through the earth and a tube of air and supplies was being passed to the miners. This is the work of the intercessor—drilling a hole of positive faith by positive prayer through the barriers of doubt, troublesome thoughts and sin that shroud the one to whom we pray, that the sunshine of God's love may bear in upon him.

Intercession is perhaps the greatest ministry in all the world. Only time will reveal what has been wrought by the prayers of the saints of God all over the world whose names have never been heralded before the public.

John Bisagno

Our Divine Prayer Partners

Because Jesus lives forever, he has a permanent priesthood. Therefore he is able to save completely those who come to God through him, because he always lives to intercede for them.

Such a high priest meets our need—one who is holy, blameless, pure, set apart from sinners, exalted above the heavens. Unlike the other high priests, he does not need to offer sacrifices day after day, first for his own sins, and then for the sins of the people. He sacrificed for their sins once for all when he offered himself. For the law appoints as high priests men who are weak; but the oath, which came after the law, appointed the Son, who has been made perfect forever.

The point of what we are saying is this: We do have such a high priest, who sat down at the right hand of the throne of the Majesty in heaven, and who serves in the sanctuary, the true tabernacle set up by the Lord, not by man.

Hebrews *7:24 — 8:2*

Our prayers ascend to God, mingled and blended with the ascending incense of the Saviour's merit. Our voices before they reach the ear of God fall in and blend with the voice of Him whom the Father heareth always.

Herbert Lockyer

In the same way, the Spirit helps us in our weakness. We do not know what we ought to pray for, but the Spirit himself intercedes for us with groans that words cannot express. And he who searches our hearts knows the mind of the Spirit, because the Spirit intercedes for the saints in accordance with God's will.

Romans *8:26-27*

Our loving Savior and the tender Holy Spirit plead in interceding prayer for the broken lives, broken homes, and the tragedies of sin and injustice throughout the world. They long for you to join them. God the Son is your enthroned Prayer Partner and God the Spirit is your indwelling Prayer Partner.

God the Father wants someone to intercede for everyone in need. God hears the cry of the orphan, the sob of the brokenhearted, the angry words of the violent, and the screams of their victims. God feels the woes of the prisoners and refugees, the hunger pangs of those starving for food. He is touched by the sorrow of those who mourn, the helplessness and hopelessness of those chained by habits of sin.

It is the special role of the Holy spirit to give you a prayer burden for all these needs and all these needy ones. God wants to express His longing love through you as you pray.

Wesley L. Duewel

A Mighty Engine

Intercessory prayer is the sweetest prayer God ever hears. What wonders it has wrought! Intercessory prayer has stopped plagues. It removed the darkness that rested over Egypt, drove away the frogs that leaped upon the land, scattered the lice and locusts that plagued the inhabitants of Zoan, removed the thunder and lightning, stayed all the ravages that God's avenging hand did upon Pharaoh and his people. We know that intercessory prayer healed diseases in the early church. We have evidence of it in old Mosaic times. When Miriam was smitten with leprosy, Moses prayed and the leprosy was removed. Intercessory prayer has raised the dead, for Elijah stretched himself upon the child seven times, and the child sneezed, and the child's soul returned. As to how many souls intercessory prayer has instrumentally saved, only eternity shall reveal it! There is nothing that intercessory prayer cannot do. Believer, you have a mighty engine in your hand—use it well, use it constantly, use it now with faith, and you shall surely prevail.

Charles Spurgeon

Praying Hands

The story is told that around the year 1490 there were two young struggling artists who were close friends. Albrecht Dürer and Franz Knigstein were very poor and had to work to support themselves, training as artists in their spare time. However, their manual work was too demanding to allow them proper training.

In desperation, they at last decided that they should cast lots to decide which of them should carry on working to support the other in art school. Albrecht won the toss, so he went off to spend time with famous artists in training, while Franz worked extra hard to support them both.

Eventually, Albrecht returned to relieve his friend. Because he had become successful as an artist, he would now be able to send Franz off to the school. But to his horror, Albrecht discovered that the heavy manual work had ruined Franz's hands forever.

One day, Albrecht fround Franz on his kness, his hands clasped in prayer, gnarled and yet offered to God in loving sacrifice. Hurriedly, Durer sketched the moment and produced a symbol for the meaning of prayer. Ever since, the intercessory prayer symbolized by that etching reminds us that prayer and friendship go together. The person to whom we pray had his hands pierced on our behalf.

James Houston

How lovely is your dwelling place,
O LORD Almighty!
My soul yearns, even faints,
for the courts of the LORD;
my heart and my flesh cry out
for the living God.

Even the sparrow has found a home,
and the swallow a nest for herself,
where she may have her young—
a place near your altar,
O LORD Almighty, my King and my God.
Blessed are those who dwell in your house;
they are ever praising you.

Psalm *84:1-4*

Pray for Your Enemies

"You have heard that it was said, 'Love your neighbor and hate your enemy.' But I tell you: Love your enemies and pray for those who persecute you, that you may be sons of your Father in heaven. He causes his sun to rise on the evil and the good, and sends rain on the righteous and the unrighteous. If you love those who love you, what reward will you get? Are not even the tax collectors doing that? And if you greet only your brothers, what are you doing more than others? Do not even pagans do that? Be perfect, therefore, as your heavenly Father is perfect.

Matthew 5:43- 48

Almighty and tender Lord Jesus Christ,
Just as I have asked you to love my friends
So I ask the same for my enemies.
You alone, Lord, are mighty.
You alone are merciful.
Give it to them.
And give the same back to me.
If I ever ask for them anything
Which is outside your perfect rule of love,
Whether through weakness, ignorance or malice,
Good Lord, do not give it to them
And do not give it back to me.
You who are the true light, lighten their darkness.
You who are the whole truth, correct their errors.
You who are the incarnate word, give life to their
souls.
Tender Lord Jesus.
Let me not be a stumbling block to them
Nor a rock of offence.
My sin is sufficient to me, without harming others.
I, a slave to sin,
Beg your mercy on my fellow slaves.
Let them be reconciled with you,
And through you reconciled to me.

                              Anselm of Canterbury

The Prayer of Adoration

One generation will commend your works to another;
  they will tell of your mighty acts.
They will speak of the glorious splendor of your
majesty,
  and I will meditate on your wonderful works.
They will tell of the power of your awesome works,
  and I will proclaim your great deeds.
They will celebrate your abundant goodness
  and joyfully sing of your righteousness.
All you have made will praise you, O LORD;
  your saints will extol you.
They will tell of the glory of your kingdom
  and speak of your might,
so that all men may know of your mighty acts
  and the glorious splendor of your kingdom.
My mouth will speak in praise of the LORD.
  Let every creature praise his holy name
  for ever and ever.

Psalm 145:4–7, 10–12, 21

Praise ye the Lord, the Almighty, the King of creation!
O my soul, praise Him, for He is thy health and salvation!
All ye who hear, now to His temple draw near;
Join me in glad adoration!
Praise ye the Lord! O let all that is in me adore Him!
All that hath life and breath, come now with praises
before Him!
Let the Amen sound from His people again:
Gladly for aye we adore Him.

Joaqhim Neander

It is good to praise the LORD
and make music to your name, O Most High,
to proclaim your love in the morning
and your faithfulness at night,
to the music of the ten-stringed lyre
and the melody of the harp.

For you make me glad by your deeds, O LORD,
I sing for joy at the works of your hands.

Psalm *92:1-4*

Prayer Changes Things

Prayer changes things, not because it is a magical formula but because behind it is nothing less than the exercise of the Creator's power. Prayer moves the hand that holds the universe. God places himself at our disposal not because he is cowed by us or our demands but because he chooses to do so. There is more to our asking than we can ever imagine, because there is more to God than we can ever fathom.

Timothy Jones

On some unmarked day…at some unnoted hour…a God-placed instinct in human hearts came alive. People sensed that if you are in trouble and you call out to God, he will answer you! He will intervene in your situation.

I can imagine one woman saying to another, "Have you heard about the God who answers when you call on him? He's more than just the Creator; he cares and responds to our needs. He actually understands what we're feeling."

"What are you talking about? God does whatever he pleases; people can't influence him one way or the other." "No, no, you're wrong. When you call out to him, he doesn't turn a deaf ear. He listens! He responds. He acts."

Jim Cymbala

How God works in answer to prayer is a mystery that
logic cannot penetrate, but that He does work in
answer to prayer is gloriously true.

Oswald Chambers

God does not give as we do, a mere handout to the
beggar, but He gives His wealth by handfuls. This is
the divine habit. He not only redeems His promises,
but when He might meet them in silver He prefers to
pay them in gold.

Charles Spurgeon

I waited patiently for the LORD;
he turned to me and heard my cry.
He lifted me out of the slimy pit,
out of the mud and mire;
he set my feet on a rock
and gave me a firm place to stand.
He put a new song in my mouth,
a hymn of praise to our God.
Many will see and fear
and put their trust in the LORD.

Psalm 40:1-3

Agents of Blessing

Through prayer you can give your love, your very self to any person, group of people, or nation. Prayer is the only expression of love which cannot be stopped or rejected.

Prayer can give you instant entrance into any home, any hospital, any government office, any courtroom in any part of the world. Just as distance cannot hinder your reach or touch in prayer, neither walls nor "no entry" signs can halt your presence or stay your hand in prayer.

The greatest way in which Christians can mediate blessing is through prayer. We have the opportunity to pray for those we can contact in no other way. From our family and closest friends whom we see often, to those we may meet but once or only hear about—we can be God's agents of blessing.

Wesley L. Duewel

How I praise Thee, precious Saviour,
That Thy love laid hold of me;
Thou hast saved and cleansed and filled me
That I might Thy channel be.
Channels only, blessed Master,
But with all Thy wondrous pow'r
Flowing thro' us,
Thou canst use us
Every day and ev'ry hour

Mary E. Maxwell

Prayer, like almost everything else, is being scrutinized by science. Some scientists and physicians have begun to acknowledge that petitionary prayer, in which one prays for oneself, has positive, healthful effects, but many of them add that this is due *only* to psychological factors such as positive thinking, expectaion, and self-suggestion. Some of these same scientists tend to believe that intercessory or distant prayer cannot possibly be effective; the mind cannot reach out, whether of its own accord or through a Supreme Being, to make things happen at a distance. If we believe in distant prayer, they say, we are fooling ourselves. But when put to the test in actual experiments in hospitals, clinics, and laboratories, distant prayer *does* have an effect—even when the recipient of the prayer is unaware the prayer is being offered.

Larry Dossey, M.D.

Transforming Grace

To pray is to change. This is a great grace. How good of God to provide a path whereby our lives can be taken over by love…joy…peace…patience…kindness….

Richard J. Foster

Prayer is like the heartbeat of the mother-with-child. Through God's influence, that constant heartbeat, we are shaped and grow into his image. A life without prayer is probably the greatest impoverishment we can experience. A life without prayer and without God would be like an unborn child vibrating to the mechanical beat of an electric clock.

Prayer develops us as whole people before God. To pray to God is to be a complete person before God, a person as God has always intended us to be. It is to be open, to confess, to be forgiven, cleansed, humbled, obedient, sustained, guided, strengthened, and daily renewed and inspired. Prayer radically transforms broken people into new people—people newly created by God. We become the unique person that God originally created each of us to be.

James Houston

If anyone is in Christ, he is a new creation; the old has gone, the new has come!

2 Corinthians 5:17

When I was at my lowest, confounded by obstacles, bewildered by the darkness that surrounded us, I discovered an astonishing truth: God is attracted to weakness. He can't resist those who humbly and honestly admit how desperately they need him. Our weakness, in fact, makes room for his power.

Jim Cymbala

Since prayer places our intellect in the brilliance of God's light and exposes our will to the warmth of his heavenly love, nothing else so effectively purifies our intellect of ignorance and our will of depraved affections. It is a stream of holy water that flows forth and makes the plants of our good desires grow green and flourish and quenches the passions within our hearts.

St. Francis de Sales

Father, into the depths of my need—my sin, my loneliness, my guilt, my failure, my inadequacy—let down the rope of your redemption and pull me to the heights where I may live completed and whole in Jesus Christ. *Amen.*

Eugene H. Peterson

The Pause that Empowers

Prayer is the pause that empowers. It is the one weapon our enemy, the devil, cannot duplicate or counterfeit.

Joni Eareckson Tada

As we go through the day we pause, when agitated or doubtful, and ask for the right thought or action. We constantly remind ourselves we are no longer running the show, humbly saying to ourselves many times each day "Thy will be done." We are then in much less danger of excitement, fear, anger, worry, self-pity, or foolish decisions. We become much more efficient. We do not tire so easily, for we are not burning up energy foolishly as we did when were trying to arrange life to suit ourselves. It works—it really does.

Alcoholics Anonymous

God wants us to make ourselves available to Him, and to say before we start to plan, "Lord, tell me what You want me to do, where You want me to go, how You want me to do it." Then our omnipotent God, with all the abundance of heaven at His disposal, will pour out His power upon us. Instead of following our tiny, tiny plans, God wants to open heaven and flood us. It's exciting.

Evelyn Christenson

Power over Darkness

If we only look for results in the earthlies when we pray, we are ill-taught. A praying saint performs far more havoc among the unseen forces of darkness than we have the slightest notion of.

Oswald Chambers

Satan's main strategy with God's people has always been to whisper, "Don't call, don't ask, don't depend on God to do great things. You'll get along fine if you just rely on your own cleverness and energy." The truth of the matter is that the devil is not terribly frightened of our human efforts and credentials. But he knows his kingdom will be damaged when we lift up our hearts to God.

Jim Cymbala

The devil smiles when we are up to our ears in work, but he trembles when we pray.

Corrie ten Boom

God shapes the world by prayer. The more praying there is in the world, the better the world will be and the mightier the forces against evil everywhere. Prayer is a disinfectant and a preventive. It purifies the air; it destroys the contagion of evil.

E. M. Bounds

Prayer reminds us that we need never despair. The one to whom we appeal is a God of justice and power and love. In prayer we participate as hopeful subversives against the powers of darkness and evil.

When your child has run away, your job has been stolen out from under you, your relationship with God has gone dry and barren, when a little boy is hounded and hurt because of the color of his skin, praying reminds us that all is not hopeless. It reminds us that even when we feel powerless, we can turn to someone who is able to do beyond our ability to think and even imagine.

Timothy Jones

Ready for the Fray

In the familiar story of David and Goliath, there is a wonderful moment when the giant gets irked at the sight of his young opponent. Goliath is genuinely insulted. "Come here,…and I'll give your flesh to the birds of the air and the beasts of the field!" he roars. Does David flinch? Does he opt for a strategic retreat behind some tree or boulder, thinking maybe to buy a little time? Absolutely not.

"As the Philistine moved closer to attack him, *David ran quickly toward the battle line to meet him.*" That is the picture of what God wants for us today: *running toward the fray!*

David's weaponry was ridiculous: a sling and five stones. It didn't matter. God still uses foolish tools in the hands of weak people to build his kingdom. Backed by prayer and his power, we can accomplish the unthinkable.

Jim Cymbala

Wonder–Working Power

The history of past revivals portrays this truth with full color. Whether you study the great Awakening, the Second Great Awakening, the Welsh Revival, the 1906 outpouring on Azusa Street in Los Angeles, or any other period of revival, you always find men and women who first inwardly groan, longing to see the status quo changed—in themselves and in their churches. They begin to call on God with insistence; prayer begets revival, which begets more prayer. It's like Psalm 80, where Asaph bemoans the sad state of his time, the broken walls, the rampaging animals, the burnt vineyards. Then in verse 18 he pleads, "Revive us, and we will call on your name."

The Holy Spirit is the Spirit of prayer. Only when we are full of the Spirit do we feel the need for God everywhere we turn. We can be driving a car, and spontaneously our spirit starts going up to God with needs and petitions and intercessions right there in the middle of traffic.

Jim Cymbala

Would you do service for Jesus your King?
There's pow'r in the blood, pow'r in the blood;
Would you live daily His praises to sing?
There's wonderful pow'r in the blood.
There is pow'r, pow'r, wonder-working pow'r
In the blood of the Lamb.

L. E. Jones

Prayer can transcend the "laws of nature." Prayer can bring God's miracle answers to man's desperate needs. It would be useless to pray for many problem situations if this were not true. If there are limits to what God can do when we pray, then prayer is playing games with God, trifling with human need, and deceiving ourselves. No! Never! Prayer is as real as God is real. There is absolutely nothing that God cannot do if it will advance His kingdom and is in accord with His will. Prayer releases God's power.

Thus prayer always has the possibility to cooperate with God's eternal purpose and to secure the miracle power of God. He does not guarantee a miracle, but God is always open to our prayer for His will to prevail for His glory. Prayer is God's ordained way to bring His miracle power to bear in human need.

Wesley L. Duewel

Ah, Sovereign LORD, you have made the heavens and the earth by your great power and outstretched arm. Nothing is too hard for you.

Jeremiah *32:17*

The
Bible's
Great
Pray-ers

God's Prayer Book

A perusal of all the prayers in the Bible brings us a
sigh of relief. For we find in them the same human
qualities we bring to this most holy of actions: whin-
ing, questioning, sighing, crying, laughing, thanking,
asking, and praising.

Janet Kobobel Grant

Give ear to my words, O LORD,
    consider my sighing.
Listen to my cry for help,
    my King and my God,
    for to you I pray.
In the morning, O LORD, you hear my voice;
    in the morning I lay my requests before you
    and wait in expectation.
I, by your great mercy,
    will come into your house;
  in reverence will I bow down
    toward your holy temple.
Lead me, O LORD, in your righteousness…
    make straight your way before me.
Let all who take refuge in you be glad;
    let them ever sing for joy.
  Spread your protection over them,
    that those who love your name may rejoice in you.
For surely, O LORD, you bless the righteous;
    you surround them with your favor as with a shield.

Psalm 5:1-3, 7-8, 11-12

How those holy [people] of old could storm the battle-ments above! When there was no way to look but *up*, they lifted up their eyes to the God who made the hills, with unshakeable confidence. At times their approach to God was both unusually familiar and dar-ing, but they were heard in that they feared.

Prayer, to [them], was more than the recital of well-known and well-worn phrases—it was the outpouring of the heart. Beset by perils, persecutions, pain and pri-vations, they naturally turned to God in their need, believing that He was able to redeem them out of all their troubles. If they knew little of the philosophy of prayer, they certainly knew a great deal about its power.

Herbert Lockyer

The LORD is my strength and my song;
he has become my salvation.
He is my God, and I will praise him,
my father's God, and I will exalt him.
The LORD is a warrior;
the LORD is his name. . . .

Who among the gods is like you, O LORD?
Who is like you—
majestic in holiness,
awesome in glory,
working wonders? . . .

In your unfailing love you will lead
the people you have redeemed.
In your strength you will guide them
to your holy dwelling.

                    Exodus *15:2–3, 11, 13*

Say "Thank You"

Praise the LORD.

Give thanks to the LORD, for he is good;
his love endures forever.
Who can proclaim the mighty acts of the LORD
or fully declare his praise? . . .

Save us, O LORD our God,
and gather us from the nations,
that we may give thanks to your holy name
and glory in your praise.

Praise be to the LORD, the God of Israel,
from everlasting to everlasting.
Let all the people say, "Amen!"

Praise the LORD.

Psalm *106:1-2, 47-48*

Hannah's Lament

Human sorrow is the birth-pang of prayer.
Herbert Lockyer

Hannah was a desperate woman. Year after year when she packed for the annual trip to Shiloh with her husband, Elkanah, her heart filled with dread. There they would present sacrifices and offerings to the Lord in His house. There they would celebrate Jehovah's goodness to them. There, once again, Hannah would feel humiliated.

"But why?" asked Elkanah. "Why are you so sad?"

Hannah tried to explain, for she deeply loved her husband, but the words jumbled, and her eyes puddled with tears.

With her head tucked under his chin, she sobbed, "I speak to the Lord, and He does not talk back to me. Nor does He answer my pleas for a child."

Elkanah sighed and kissed the top of Hannah's head. "Don't I mean more to you than ten sons?" he asked quietly.

"You are everything a husband can mean to a wife," she answered. "But I cannot extinguish my desire to conceive. It burns within me."

Judith C. Couchman

In bitterness of soul Hannah wept much and prayed to the LORD. And she made a vow, saying, "O LORD Almighty, if you will only look upon your servant's misery and remember me, and not forget your servant but give her a son, then I will give him to the LORD for all the days of his life.". . .

Early the next morning they arose and worshiped before the LORD and then went back to their home at Ramah. Elkanah lay with Hannah his wife, and the LORD remembered her. So in the course of time Hannah conceived and gave birth to a son. She named him Samuel, saying, "Because I asked the LORD for him."

After he was weaned, she took the boy with her, young as he was . . . and brought him to the house of the LORD. . . . They brought the boy to Eli, and she said to him, "As surely as you live, my lord, I am the woman who stood here beside you praying to the LORD. I prayed for this child, and the LORD has grant-ed me what I asked of him. So now I give him to the LORD. For his whole life he will be given over to the LORD."

1 Samuel *1: 10-11, 19-20, 24-28*

The God of Sorrows

He was despised and rejected by men,
   a man of sorrows, and familiar with suffering.

Isaiah 53:3

Do you have sleepless nights, tossing on the hot pillow,
and watching for the first glint of
dawn? Ask the divine Spirit to enable you to fix your
thoughts on God your Maker, and
believe that He can fill those lonely, dreary hours with song.
Is yours the night of bereavement? Is it not often at such
a time that God draws near,
and assures the mourner that the Lord has need of the
departed loved one, and called "the
eager, earnest spirit to stand in the bright throng of the
invisible, liberated, radiant, active,
intent on some high mission"; and as the thought enters,
is there not the beginning of a song?
Is yours the night of discouragement and fancied or actual
failure? No one
understands you, your friends reproach; but your Maker
draws nigh, and gives you a
song—a song of hope, the song which is harmonious with
the strong, deep music of His
providence. Be ready to sing the songs your Maker gives.
                    Selected

A Servant's Supplication

O LORD, God of heaven, the great and awesome God, who keeps his covenant of love with those who love him and obey his commands, let your ear be attentive and your eyes open to hear the prayer your servant is praying before you day and night for your servants, the people of Israel. I confess the sins we Israelites, including myself and my father's house, have committed against you. We have acted very wickedly toward you. We have not obeyed the commands, decrees and laws you gave your servant Moses.

Remember the instruction you gave your servant Moses, saying, "If you are unfaithful, I will scatter you among the nations, but if you return to me and obey my commands, then even if your exiled people are at the farthest horizon, I will gather them from there and bring them to the place I have chosen as a dwelling for my Name."

They are your servants and your people, whom you redeemed by your great strength and your mighty hand. O LORD, let your ear be attentive to the prayer of this your servant and to the prayer of your servants who delight in revering your name.

Nehemiah 1:5–11

Jesus, how sweet is the very thought of you! You fill my heart with joy. The sweetness of your love surpasses the sweetness of honey. Nothing sweeter than you can be described; no words can express the joy of your love. Only those who have tasted your love for themselves can comprehend it. In your love you listen to all my prayers, even when my wishes are childish, my words confused, and my thoughts foolish. And you answer my prayers, not according to my own misdirected desires, which would bring only bitter misery, but according to my real needs, which brings me sweet joy. Thank you, Jesus, for giving yourself to me.
Bernard of Clairvaux

The Great Intercessor

"I have seen these people," the LORD said to Moses, "and they are a stiff-necked people. Now leave me alone so that my anger may burn against them and that I may destroy them. Then I will make you into a great nation."

But Moses sought the favor of the LORD his God. "O LORD," he said, "why should your anger burn against your people, whom you brought out of Egypt with great power and a mighty hand? Why should the Egyptians say, 'It was with evil intent that he brought them out, to kill them in the mountains and to wipe them off the face of the earth'? Turn from your fierce anger; relent and do not bring disaster on your people. Remember your servants Abraham, Isaac and Israel, to whom you swore by your own self: 'I will make your descendants as numerous as the stars in the sky and I will give your descendants all this land I promised them, and it will be their inheritance forever.'" Then the LORD relented and did not bring on his people the disaster he had threatened.

Exodus *32:9-14*

Praises to the King of Kings

Then King David went in and sat before the LORD, and he said:

"Who am I, O LORD God, and what is my family, that you have brought me this far? And as if this were not enough in your sight, O God, you have spoken about the future of the house of your servant. You have looked on me as though I were the most exalted of men, O LORD God.

"What more can David say to you for honoring your servant? For you know your servant, O LORD. For the sake of your servant and according to your will, you have done this great thing and made known all these great promises.

"There is no one like you, O LORD, and there is no God but you, as we have heard with our own ears. And who is like your people Israel—the one nation on earth whose God went out to redeem a people for himself, and to make a name for yourself, and to perform great and awesome wonders by driving out nations from before your people, whom you redeemed from Egypt? You made your people Israel your very own forever, and you, O LORD, have become their God.

"And now, LORD, let the promise you have made concerning your servant and his house be established forever. Do as you promised, so that it will be established and that your name will be great forever. Then men will say, 'The LORD Almighty, the God over Israel, is Israel's God!' And the house of your servant David will be established before you.

"You, my God, have revealed to your servant that you will build a house for him. So your servant has found courage to pray to you. O LORD, you are God! You have promised these good things to your servant. Now you have been pleased to bless the house of your servant, that it may continue forever in your sight; for you, O LORD, have blessed it, and it will be blessed forever."

1 Chronicles *17:16–27*

O LORD, God of our fathers, are you not the God who is in heaven? You rule over all the kingdoms of the nations. Power and might are in your hand, and no one can withstand you.

2 Chronicles *20:6*

Healing Prayers

See now that I myself am He!
There is no god besides me.
I put to death and I bring to life,
I have wounded and I will heal,
and no one can deliver out of my hand.

Deuteronomy *32:39*

In those days Hezekiah became ill and was at the point
of death. The prophet Isaiah son of Amoz went to him
and said, "This is what the LORD says: Put your house
in order, because you are going to die; you will not
recover."

Hezekiah turned his face to the wall and prayed to the
LORD, "Remember, O LORD, how I have walked
before you faithfully and with wholehearted devotion
and have done what is good in your eyes." And
Hezekiah wept bitterly.

Then the word of the LORD came to Isaiah: "Go and
tell Hezekiah, 'This is what the LORD, the God of
your father David, says: I have heard your prayer and
seen your tears; I will add fifteen years to your life.
And I will deliver you and this city from the hand of
the king of Assyria. I will defend this city.'"

Isaiah *38:1-6*

Some time later the son of the woman who owned the house became ill. He grew worse and worse, and finally stopped breathing. She said to Elijah, "What do you have against me, man of God? Did you come to remind me of my sin and kill my son?"

"Give me your son," Elijah replied. He took him from her arms, carried him to the upper room where he was staying, and laid him on his bed. Then he cried out to the LORD, "O LORD my God, have you brought tragedy also upon this widow I am staying with, by causing her son to die?" Then he stretched himself out on the boy three times and cried to the LORD, "O LORD my God, let this boy's life return to him!"

The LORD heard Elijah's cry, and the boy's life returned to him, and he lived. Elijah picked up the child and carried him down from the room into the house. He gave him to his mother and said, "Look, your son is alive!"

Then the woman said to Elijah, "Now I know that you are a man of God and that the word of the LORD from your mouth is the truth."

1 Kings *17:17-24*

A Whale of a Prayer

From inside the fish Jonah prayed to the LORD his God. He said:

"In my distress I called to the LORD,
and he answered me.
From the depths of the grave I called for help,
and you listened to my cry.
You hurled me into the deep,
into the very heart of the seas,
and the currents swirled about me;
all your waves and breakers
swept over me.
I said, 'I have been banished
from your sight;
yet I will look again
toward your holy temple.'
The engulfing waters threatened me,
the deep surrounded me;
seaweed was wrapped around my head.
To the roots of the mountains I sank down;
the earth beneath barred me in forever.
But you brought my life up from the pit,
O LORD my God.

"When my life was ebbing away,
I remembered you, LORD,
and my prayer rose to you,
to your holy temple.

"Those who cling to worthless idols
forfeit the grace that could be theirs.
But I, with a song of thanksgiving,
will sacrifice to you.
What I have vowed I will make good.
Salvation comes from the LORD."
 And the LORD commanded the fish, and it vomited
Jonah onto dry land.

Jonah 2

Asaph's Memories

I cried out to God for help;
I cried out to God to hear me.
When I was in distress, I sought the Lord;
at night I stretched out untiring hands
and my soul refused to be comforted.

I remembered you, O God, and I groaned;
I mused, and my spirit grew faint.

You kept my eyes from closing;
I was too troubled to speak.
I thought about the former days,
the years of long ago;
I remembered my songs in the night.
My heart mused and my spirit inquired:

"Will the Lord reject forever?
Will he never show his favor again?
Has his unfailing love vanished forever?
Has his promise failed for all time?
Has God forgotten to be merciful?
Has he in anger withheld his compassion?"

Then I thought, "To this I will appeal:
the years of the right hand of the Most High."
I will remember the deeds of the LORD;
yes, I will remember your miracles of long ago.
I will meditate on all your works
and consider all your mighty deeds.

Your ways, O God, are holy.
What god is so great as our God?
You are the God who performs miracles;
you display your power among the peoples.
With your mighty arm you redeemed your people,
the descendants of Jacob and Joseph.

The waters saw you, O God,
the waters saw you and writhed;
the very depths were convulsed.
The clouds poured down water,
the skies resounded with thunder;
your arrows flashed back and forth.
Your thunder was heard in the whirlwind,
your lightning lit up the world;
the earth trembled and quaked.
Your path led through the sea,
your way through the mighty waters,
though your footprints were not seen.

You led your people like a flock
by the hand of Moses and Aaron.

Psalm 77

A Virgin's Song
of Joy

The angel went to [Mary] and said, "Greetings, you who are highly favored! The Lord is with you." Mary was greatly troubled at his words and wondered what kind of greeting this might be. But the angel said to her, "Do not be afraid, Mary, you have found favor with God. You will be with child and give birth to a son, and you are to give him the name Jesus. He will be great and will be called the Son of the Most High. The Lord God will give him the throne of his father David, and he will reign over the house of Jacob forever; his kingdom will never end."

"How will this be," Mary asked the angel, "since I am a virgin?" The angel answered, "The Holy Spirit will come upon you, and the power of the Most High will overshadow you. So the holy one to be born will be called the Son of God. Even Elizabeth your relative is going to have a child in her old age, and she who was said to be barren is in her sixth month. For nothing is impossible with God." "I am the Lord's servant," Mary answered. "May it be to me as you have said.". . .

And Mary said:

"My soul glorifies the Lord
and my spirit rejoices in God my Savior,
for he has been mindful
of the humble state of his servant.
From now on all generations will call me blessed,
for the Mighty One has done great things for me—
holy is his name.
His mercy extends to those who fear him,
from generation to generation.
He has performed mighty deeds with his arm;
he has scattered those who are proud in their inmost
thoughts.
He has brought down rulers from their thrones
but has lifted up the humble.
He has filled the hungry with good things
but has sent the rich away empty.
He has helped his servant Israel,
remembering to be merciful
to Abraham and his descendants forever,
even as he said to our fathers."

Luke 1:28–38, 46–55

Fire Power

In Acts 4, when the apostles were unjustly arrested, imprisoned, and threatened, they didn't call for a protest; they didn't reach for some political leverage. Instead, they headed to a prayer meeting. Soon the place was vibrating with the power of the Holy Spirit.

Jim Cymbala

The priests and the captain of the temple guard and the Sadducees came up to Peter and John while they were speaking to the people. They were greatly disturbed because the apostles were teaching the people and proclaiming in Jesus the resurrection of the dead. They seized Peter and John, and because it was evening, they put them in jail until the next day. . . .

When they saw the courage of Peter and John and realized that they were unschooled, ordinary men, they were astonished and they took note that these men had been with Jesus. . . . "What are we going to do with these men?" they asked. "Everybody living in Jerusalem knows they have done an outstanding miracle, and we cannot deny it. But to stop this thing from spreading any further among the people, we must warn these men to speak no longer to anyone in this name."

Then they called them in again and commanded them not to speak or teach at all in the name of Jesus. But Peter and John replied, "Judge for yourselves whether it is right in God's sight to obey you rather than God. For we cannot help speaking about what we have seen and heard." After further threats they let them go. . . .

On their release, Peter and John went back to their own people and reported all that the chief priests and elders had said to them. When they heard this, they raised their voices together in prayer to God. "Sovereign Lord," they said, "you made the heaven and the earth and the sea, and everything in them. . . . Now, Lord, enable your servants to speak your word with great boldness. Stretch out your hand to heal and perform miraculous signs and wonders through the name of your holy servant Jesus."

After they prayed, the place where they were meeting was shaken. And they were all filled with the Holy Spirit and spoke the word of God boldly. . . . With great power the apostles continued to testify to the resurrection of the Lord Jesus, and much grace was upon them all.

Acts 4:1-3, 13, 16-21, 23-24, 29-31, 33

Praise the Lord!

I will sing of the LORD's great love forever;
with my mouth I will make your faithfulness known
through all generations.
I will declare that your love stands firm forever,
that you established your faithfulness in heaven itself.

The heavens praise your wonders, O LORD,
your faithfulness too, in the assembly of the holy ones.
For who in the skies above can compare with the
LORD?
Who is like the LORD among the heavenly beings?
In the council of the holy ones God is greatly feared;
he is more awesome than all who surround him.
O LORD God Almighty, who is like you?
You are mighty, O LORD, and your faithfulness sur-
rounds you.

You rule over the surging sea;
when its waves mount up, you still them.
You crushed Rahab like one of the slain;
with your strong arm you scattered your enemies.
The heavens are yours, and yours also the earth;
you founded the world and all that is in it.
You created the north and the south;
Tabor and Hermon sing for joy at your name.
Your arm is endued with power;
your hand is strong, your right hand exalted.

Psalm *89:1-2, 5-13*

Praise the LORD.

Praise God in his sanctuary;
praise him in his mighty heavens.
Praise him for his acts of power;
praise him for his surpassing greatness.
Praise him with the sounding of the trumpet,
praise him with the harp and lyre,
praise him with tambourine and dancing,
praise him with the strings and flute,
praise him with the clash of cymbals,
praise him with resounding cymbals.

Let everything that has breath praise the LORD.

Praise the LORD.

Psalm *150*

Sources

Alcoholics Anonymous (New York: Alcoholics Anonymous World Services, Inc., 1976).

The excerpt from the book Alcoholics Anonymous, pages 87-88, is reprinted with permission of Alcoholics Anonymous World Services, Inc. Permission to use this excerpt does not mean that A.A. necessarily agrees with the views expressed herin. A.A. is a program of recovery from alcoholism only—use of this excerpt in connection with programs and activities which are patterned after A.A., but which address other problems, or in any other non-A.A. context, does not imply otherwise.

John Bisagno, *The Power of Positive Praying* (Grand Rapids, MI: Zondervan PublishingHouse, 1965).

E.M. Bounds, *E. M. Bounds on Prayer* © 1997. Used by permission of Whitaker House, 30 Hunt Valley Circle, New Kensington, PA 15068.

Bill Bright, *How You Can Pray with Confidence* (Orlando, FL: New Life Publications, 1971).

Frederick Buechner, *Listening to Your Life* (New York: HarperSanFrancisco, 1992).

Amy Carmichael, *A Very Present Help* (Ann Arbor, MI: Servant Publications, 1996).

Michael Casey, *Toward God: The Ancient Wisdom of Western Prayer,* (Liguori, MO: Triumph Books, 1996).

Oswald Chambers, This material is taken from *Prayer: A Holy Occupation,* by Oswald Chambers, edited by

Harry Verploegh. © 1993 by the Oswald Chambers Publications Assoc. Ltd, and is used by permission of Discovery House Publishers, Box 3566, Grand Rapids, MI 49501. All rights reserved.

Evelyn Christenson, *A Journey into Prayer* (Colorado Springs, CO: Chariot Victor Publishing, 1995).

Clare Cloninger, *Dear Abba*, by Clare Cloninger, © 1997, Word Publishing, Nashville, TN. All rights reserved.

Judy C. Couchman, (compiler), *Breakfast for the Soul: Spiritual Nourishment to Start Your Day* (Tulsa, OK: Honor Books, 1998). *His Gentle Voice: Listening for God in Everyday Moments* (Sisters, OR: Multnomah Publishers, Inc., 1998).

Jim Cymbala, *Fresh Wind, Fresh Fire: What Happens When God's Spirit Invades the Hearts of His People* (Grand Rapids, MI: ZondervanPublishingHouse, 1997).

Dudley J. Delffs, Reprinted from *The Prayer Centered Life,* © 1997 by Dudley J. Delffs. Used by permission of NavPress, Colorado Springs, CO. All rights reserved. For copies call (800) 366-7788.

Linda Dillow, *Calm My Anxious Heart* (Colorado Springs, CO: NavPress Publishing Group, 1998).

Brian J. Dodd, *Praying Jesus' Way* (Downers Grove, IL: InterVarsity Press, 1997).

Larry Dossey, M.D., *Prayer is Good Medicine,* © 1996 by Larry Dossey, M.D. Reprinted with permission of HarperCollins Publishers, Inc.

Wesley L. Duewel, *Touch the World Through Prayer,* (Grand Rapids, MI: ZondervanPublishingHouse, 1986).

John Fischer, *True Believers Don't Ask Why,* (Minneapolis, MN: Bethany House Publishers, 1989). Used by permission.

Richard J. Foster, *Celebration of Discipline* © 1978 by Richard J. Foster. Reprinted with permission of HarperCollins Publishers, Inc. *Prayer: Finding the Heart's True Home* © 1992 by Richard J. Foster. Reprinted with permission of HarperCollins Publishers, Inc.

Ken Gire (compiler), *Between Heaven and Earth* (New York: HarperSanFrancisco, 1997).

Janet Kobobel Grant, *Growing in Prayer* (Grand Rapids, MI: ZondervanPublishingHouse, 1998).

Thomas H. Green, S.J., *Opening to God: A Guide to Prayer* (Notre Dame, IN: Ave Maria Press, 1977).

Emilie Griffin, *Clinging: The Experience of Prayer* (San Francisco, CA: Harper & Row, Publishers, 1984).

Steve Harper, *Praying Through the Lord's Prayer* (Nashville, TN: Upper Room Books, 1992).

Jack Hayford, *Prayer is Invading the Impossible,* © 1977, Bridge-Logos Publishers, North Brunswick, NJ.

James Houston, *The Transforming Power of Prayer* (Colorado Springs, CO: NavPress Publishing Group, 1996).

David Jeremiah, *Prayer: The Great Adventure* (Sisters, OR, Multnomah Publishers, Inc., 1997).

Timothy Jones, From *The Art of Prayer* by Timothy Jones. Copyright © 1995 by Timothy Jones. Reprinted by permission of Ballantine Books, a Division of Random House, Inc.

Phillip Keller, *A Layman Looks at the Lord's Prayer* (Chicago: Moody Press, 1976).

Phillip W. Keller, *A Shepherd Looks at Psalm 23* (Grand Rapids, MI: ZondervanPublishingHouse, 1970).

David and Heather Kopp, Reprinted from *Praying the Bible for Your Children*, © 1997 by David and Heather Kopp. Used by permission of WaterBrook Press, Colorado Springs, CO. All rights reserved.

Herbert Lockyer, *All the Prayers of the Bible* (Grand Rapids, MI: ZondervanPublishingHouse, 1959).

Catherine Marshall, *Adventures in Prayer*, Chosen Books, a division of Baker Book House Company, © 1975.

Andrew Murray, *Loving God with All Your Heart* (Ann Arbor, MI: Servant Publications, 1996).

Warren & Ruth Myers, *31 Days of Prayer: Moving God's Mighty Hand* (Sisters, OR: Multnomah Publishers, 1997).

Julian of Norwich, *All Will Be Well: 30 Days with a Great Spiritual Teacher* (Notre Dame, IN: Ave Maria Press, 1995).

William Carr Peel, Reprinted from *What God Does When Men Pray* © 1993 by William Carr Peel. Used by permission of NavPress, Colorado Springs, CO. All rights reserved. For copies call (800) 366-7788.

Eugene H. Peterson, *Praying with the Psalms* © 1993 by Eugene Peterson. Reprinted with permission of HarperCollins Publishers, Inc.

Pope John Paul II (Tony Castle, compiler), *The Way of Prayer,* (New York: Crossroad Publishing Company, 1995).

James & Martha Reapsome, *Effective Prayer* (Grand Rapids, MI: Zondervan Publishing House, 1992).

St. Francis de Sales, From *Introduction to the Devout Life* © 1950 by Harper & Brothers. Used by permission of Doubleday, a division of Random House, Inc.

St. Teresa of Avila, *A Life of Prayer: Faith and Passion for God Alone* (Minneapolis, MN: Bethany House Publishers, 1983).

Don Sanford, *Prayers for Every Occasion* (Grand Rapids, MI: ZondervanPublishingHouse, 1957).

Robert Schuller, *Power to Grow Beyond Yourself,* Chosen Books, a division of Baker Book House Company, © 1987.

John R. W. Stott, *Basic Christianity,* (Grand Rapids, MI: Wm. B. Eerdmans Publishing Company, 1986).

Charles Spurgeon, *Charles Spurgeon on Prayer: a 30-Day Devotional Treasury* (Lynnwood, WA: Emerald Books, 1998).

Millie Stamm, *Beside Still Waters* (Grand Rapids, MI: ZondervanPublishingHouse, 1984).

Joni Eareckson Tada, *Seeking God* (Brentwood, TN: Wolgemuth & Hyatt, Publishers, Inc. 1991).

Corrie ten Boom, *Not Good if Detached,* Fleming H. Revell, a division of Baker Book House Company, ©1999.

A. W. Tozer, From *The Knowledge of the Holy, The Attributes of God: Their Meaning in the Christian,* © 1961 by Aiden Wilson Tozer. Copyright Renewed. Reprinted by permission of HarperCollins Publishers, Inc. *The Pursuit of God,* 1982, Christian Publications, Camp Hill, PA.

Simon Tugwell, *Prayer in Practice* (Springfield, IL: Templegate Publishers, 1974).

Sheila Walsh, et al., *We Brake for Joy* (Grand Rapids, MI: ZondervanPublishingHouse, 1998).

Walter Wangerin, Jr., *Whole Prayer* (Grand Rapids, MI: ZondervanPublishingHouse, 1998).

Thelma Wells, *God Will Make a Way* (Nashville, TN: Thomas Nelson, Inc., 1998). *What's Going On, Lord?* (Nashville, TN: Thomas Nelson, Inc., 1999).

N.T. Wright. Excerpted from N.T. Wright, *The Lord and His Prayer*, © 1996 N.T. Wright, Wm. B. Eerdmans Publishing Co., Grand Rapids, MI. Reprinted by permission of the publisher, all rights reserved.

Wendy M. Wright, "Desert Listening," *Weavings* (Nashville, TN: The Upper Room), Vol. IX, Number 3, May/June, 1994.